THE

GARDENERS'

BOOK

For Chris Craig
who has always loved her garden

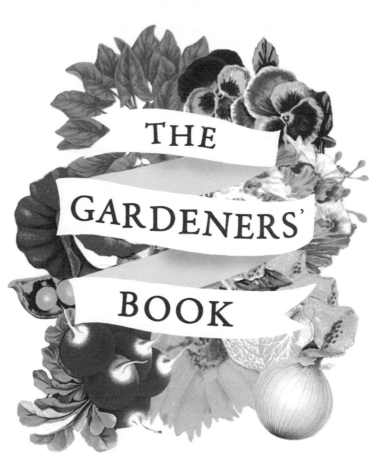

THE
GARDENERS'
BOOK

*Age-old advice and
tips for the garden*

Diana Craig

Michael O'Mara Books Limited

First published in Great Britain in 2008 by
Michael O'Mara Books Limited
9 Lion Yard
Tremadoc Road
London SW4 7NQ

This edition first published in 2012

A CIP catalogue record for this book is available from the British Library.

Papers used by Michael O'Mara Books Limited are natural, recyclable products made
from wood grown in sustainable forests. The manufacturing processes conform to the
environmental regulations of the country of origin.

ISBN: 978-1-84317-957-3

1 3 5 7 9 10 8 6 4 2

www.mombooks.com

Illustrations © David Woodroffe 2008, 2012

Cover design by Anna Morrison

Designed and typeset by www.glensaville.com

Printed and bound in Great Britain by Clays Ltd, St Ives plc

CONTENTS

INTRODUCTION

Even if you've never picked up so much as a trowel before, it's never too late to start gardening. Remember, plants *want* to grow – that is their purpose in life. All you have to do is give them a helping hand, then stand back and let them do the rest. Lack of money and space are no deterrents either. Imagination and improvisation, coupled with some old-fashioned gardener's thrift, are the way forward here.

Whether you're an experienced gardener or a novice, you will find plenty to inform and inspire in the pages that follow. Discover how to plan your garden to make the most of the space, how to grow nutritious and delicious food for you and your family, and how to do your bit for the planet by encouraging wildlife into your garden: just watching them will be reward enough as they fill your garden with vibrant life.

Learn the technical stuff – what makes for good soil, how to get more for your money by growing from seed and cuttings, and just what all those baffling gardening terms mean. Know that at last you can sleep easy at night because you now have an arsenal of nearly twenty different remedies for dealing with slugs and snails – not to mention a similar number of weapons to use in the war against Tiddles the cat, who views your new flower beds and seed trays as a convenient toilet.

And, when you've read, marked and inwardly digested . . . and dug and sowed and planted and pruned and weeded . . . sit back and relax in a comfortable chair, an ice-cold drink in hand, and watch as the sun goes down over your own personal Garden of Eden.

BACK IN THYME

|||||||||||||||||||||||||||||||||||||||||||||||||||||||||||||||||||||||||||||||||||||||||||||

Gardens have always had a special place in the human heart and are sometimes seen as mystical places where magical things can happen.

THE GARDEN OF EDEN

'And the Lord planted a garden eastward in Eden . . . and out of the ground made the Lord God to grow every tree that is pleasant to the sight, and good for food; the tree of life also in the midst of the garden, and the tree of knowledge of good and evil. And a river went out of Eden to water the garden . . .'

Perhaps the most fabled of all gardens is the Garden of Eden, the one that God himself created. The Bible tells us that it was God's custom, after the searing heat of the day, to take a refreshing stroll in his garden 'in the cool of the evening'. Picture the scene: the Divine Being walking, perhaps barefoot, over the sun-warmed grass, the hem of His garment swishing as He moves, while the river that irrigates the lush green earth ripples gently in the background.

However, it was on one such peaceful evening stroll that everything went wrong for the human race. When God discovered that Adam was hiding from him because he had realized he was naked, the Creator was furious. 'Who told thee that thou wast naked?,' he thundered. 'Hast thou eaten of the tree, whereof I commanded thee that thou shouldest not eat?' The game was up. Adam and Eve had eaten the forbidden fruit – traditionally an apple but, given the Middle East's climate, more likely a pomegranate or a fig. Adam blamed Eve and Eve blamed the Serpent, but God was having none of it. He expelled the pair forthwith, and their descendents have had to struggle with existence ever since.

PARADISE GARDENS

The Garden of Eden was a type of 'paradise garden', a kind of other-worldly space of greenery, cooling water, flowers, fruit, perfumes and birdsong, separate from the harsh reality beyond its boundaries.

The word 'paradise' comes from the old Persian, and originally referred to a walled compound or garden. The term has since become an alternative for 'heaven'.

Other paradise gardens include the Garden of the Hesperides in Greek mythology. Like Eden, this was complete with its own magical tree – an apple tree belonging to the mother goddess Hera – and serpent – the dragon Ladon set to guard the apples. The Hesperides were nymphs who tended the tree, watering it with the Water of Life.

GARDENS OF INNOCENCE

- The famous medieval tapestries known as *The Lady and the Unicorn* show a lady with a unicorn resting against her, in an enclosed flowery meadow. The unicorn was a symbol of purity and chastity and the enclosure again suggests an otherworldly paradise, untainted by the wickedness of the world.

- *The Garden of Earthly Delights* is the central panel of a triptych painted by Hieronymous Bosch (1450–1516) and, according to some scholars, depicts a lost paradise.

The kiss of the sun for pardon,
The song of the birds for mirth,
One is nearer God's heart in a garden
Than anywhere else on earth.
FROM GARDEN THOUGHTS BY
DOROTHY FRANCES GURNEY

THE HANGING GARDENS OF BABYLON

After Queen Amytis married King Nebuchadnezzar II of Babylon (modern-day Iraq) she continued to pine for her native land in green, mountainous Media, in what is now north-western Iran. In an attempt to cheer her up, her husband built for her her own green mountain. Constructed in about 600 BC and rising from the sun-baked plains, this green, leafy, artificial mound with its terraced, rooftop gardens became known as the Hanging Gardens of Babylon, one of the original Seven Wonders of the World. An extraordinary engineering feat, the gardens were, according to the Greek historian Diodorus Siculus, 122 m (400 ft) wide by 122 m (400 ft) long and more than 24 m (80 ft) in height. Another account says that slaves worked in shifts, turning screws to lift water from the nearby Euphrates River to irrigate the terraces. The gardens were destroyed by earthquakes in about the second century BC.

THE SECRET GARDEN

In the children's classic of the same name by Frances Hodgson Burnett, lonely, orphaned Mary Lennox is sent to live at her uncle's house, Misseltwhaite Manor in Yorkshire in the north of England. One day, she discovers a secret walled garden that has lain neglected for years, and she slowly starts to coax it back to life. She invites her bedridden cousin Colin to visit the garden too, and gradually, as the garden begins to flower again, so do the children – Mary becoming happy and Colin learning to walk once more. The rebirth of the garden thus becomes a metaphor for the rebirth of the children.

A GIANT'S GARDEN

In Oscar Wilde's beautiful children's story *The Selfish Giant*, the giant refuses to let children play in his garden: 'My own garden is my own garden,' he thunders. But one child who visits it without permission changes the giant's mind. This is the Christ Child. When the giant dies, He takes him to His own garden – paradise.

KNOW YOUR ONIONS

Learn the meaning of garden jargon and impress your friends by sounding really knowledgeable. Here are some terms to fling casually into any gardening conversation:

Annual A plant that does it all in one year – germinates, flowers, produces seeds and dies (dropping its seeds to kickstart the next generation).

Biennial A plant that takes two years to do its thing, germinating and growing in the first year, then flowering, seeding and dying in the second.

Bolt What you may feel like doing when faced with an untidy garden. In the case of plants, to bolt is to flower and seed prematurely.

Bulb A swollen, onion-shaped underground stem with roots which stores food for a plant.

Cordon A plant, usually a fruit tree, reduced by pruning to one main, slanting stem.

Corm A swollen underground stem similar to a bulb.

Crock A piece of broken clay pot placed over the hole at the bottom of a plant pot to aid drainage and provide air circulation to the roots.

Crop rotation A system of growing different groups of vegetables on different sections of the vegetable plot, in order to prevent the build-up of pests and diseases that affect each group. The four groups are: legumes (peas and beans); alliums (onions, leeks, garlic); roots, tubers and solanaceous crops (potatoes, carrots, tomatoes, peppers, celery, etc.); and brassicas (cabbage, cauliflower, etc.).

Cutting Part of a plant (shoot, leaf, root, bud) that is cut and propagated to grow a new plant.

Drill A narrow, straight furrow in the soil into which seeds are sown.

Espalier A plant, usually a fruit tree, trained to have one main vertical stem and three or more horizontal branches.

Friable What your soil should be – good and crumbly.

Half-hardy Used to describe plants that are not fully hardy and intolerant of frost.

Hardy Used to describe plants that can withstand year-round weather conditions outdoors, including frost, without protection.

Herbaceous Used to describe a non-woody plant whose stems die down to soil level in winter. Fling the term 'herbaceous perennial' into the conversation and watch your rating rise.

Humus Decayed vegetable matter in the soil (not the Mediterranean dip you serve with pitta bread).

Intercropping A cunning system to get more from the same plot by growing faster-maturing crops between slower ones.

Loam What all gardeners aspire to – easily worked soil with a balanced mixture of sand, clay and silt, usually rich in humus.

Perennial Any plant that lives for three or more seasons. Perennials may be herbaceous or woody.

Pollination The transfer of pollen, by insects or wind, from the anthers (the pollen-producing parts of flowers) to the stigmas (the parts that receive the pollen), leading to fertilization and the production of seed.

Propagation Different methods by which new plants are raised.

Rhizome A thick, horizontal underground stem that stores food for the plant and produces roots.

Thatch What some people have on their roofs, and what other people have on their lawns – a mat of dead organic matter mixed in with the grass.

Tilth Gorgeous stuff this – a fine, crumbly surface layer of soil that you need for sowing seeds, and that you produce by digging and raking.

Tuber Yet another swollen underground rooting stem!

Woody Used to describe plants with woody stems and branches, i.e. shrubs and trees.

GARDENERS' GEAR

It is not unheard of for people to cut the grass with scissors, to prune with a bread knife, or to dig with a kitchen fork, but life will be much easier if you buy the right tools for the job. A basic gardener's toolkit need not be expensive; the larger DIY stores usually have their own-brand budget ranges, or you could check out the prices in your local hardware shop. You can then add to your kit as the need arises.

GETTING STARTED

These items are the very least you will need to get gardening.

Fork
Used for cultivating and lifting plants, this is easier to use on heavier soils than a spade. Choose one that is the right weight and size for you.

Spade
Used in the same way as a fork, and for digging holes for planting. As with forks, choose one that is the right size for you, and not so heavy that it makes digging even harder work.

Trowel
Effectively a small spade. Narrow-bladed trowels are great for digging in very confined areas such as rock gardens and for general transplanting. Wide-bladed trowels are useful for planting out bedding plants and bulbs, especially in pots and window-boxes.

Hand fork
Useful for weeding and for lifting small plants. Like the larger version, these are great for heavier soils.

Hoe
Much too useful a tool not to have, a hoe makes short work of weeds if used regularly – hold the blade parallel to the surface of the soil and slice through their stems. Hoes can also be used to make drills in the soil for sowing seeds. They come in several varieties but for general use the Dutch hoe is a good all-rounder.

Lawnmower
Obviously only necessary if you have a lawn! Manual ones are pretty basic and need little maintenance. Powered mowers run either on mains electricity or petrol, and come as cylinder, rotary or hover types. Petrol-driven cylinders often have wider cutting widths than electric ones, which reduces mowing time, but they can be heavy to manoeuvre. Rotaries and hovers are good for slightly uneven ground or areas of long grass, but if they are electric they may overheat if there is too much long grass to scythe through. Electric mowers also have trailing leads to worry about. If you want that wonderful, stripy bowling-green effect, you'll need a mower with a back roller. Decide what your needs are, do your research and take advice before you buy. And don't forget that, once you have bought it, your mower will need regular maintenance too.

Secateurs
Essential for pruning woody stems up to about 1 cm ($^1/2$ in) thick and soft shoots of any thickness. Make sure the blades are sharp

so that you don't leave a ragged cut that may lead to infection or the whole shoot dying back.

Garden shears
Essential for cutting hedges, and generally useful for slicing through awkward patches of grass or cutting plants back at the end of the growing season.

Watering can
Available in either sturdy plastic or more expensive, traditional, galvanized metal. Metal types are heavier to carry. A good size for general use is 9 litres (2 gallons).

Hose
Necessary if you have more than pots or a tiny patch to water, and for soaking more inaccessible parts of the garden. More

expensive hoses are double-walled and reinforced, which makes them more flexible and stops them kinking: kinks in a hose interrupt the water flow and damage the hose wall. A hosepipe may be round or flat: the flat variety comes on its own reel and has to be completely unrolled before use; it may also kink unless rolled out flat, and can be difficult to rewind unless all the water is drained out.

String
Essential garden aid and can be cut to any length for tying plants to canes or stakes. To minimize rubbing or pulling on stems, tie in a figure-of-eight, with one loop knotted snugly but gently around the stem.

Gloves
Necessary for protecting your hands from dirt and thorns and general gardening exposure.

GETTING SERIOUS

Add these items as you become more proficient – and ambitious.

Rake
Used for raking soil, so only necessary if you are sowing seeds directly into the soil.

Lawn rake
Used for raking up grass cuttings, and removing moss from lawns.

Strimmer
Useful for lawn edges or longer grass.

Wheelbarrow
Only really necessary if you have largish loads to transport – and if you have space to store one. Ball-wheeled types are better for heavier loads and rough ground.

Lawn shears
Specialized cutters for trimming the edges of lawns.

Half-moon lawn edger
A half-moon bladed tool used with a rocking motion to cut away uneven lawn edges – a must-have item for those fanatical about impeccable lawns.

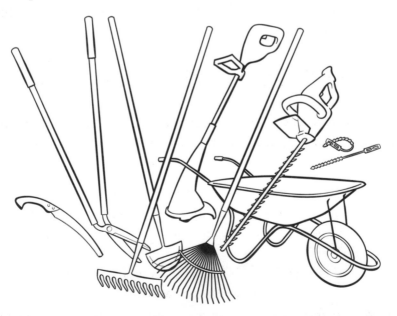

Pruning saw
Useful for cutting branches more than 2.5 cm (1 in) thick.

Plant ties
Used in the same way as garden string, these are not quite so adaptable because they come in fixed lengths and may not be long enough for the job in hand.

Power hedge-trimmer
Great for making short work of hedge-cutting, but more expensive than shears.

Lawn sprinkler
Pretty much an environmental no-no because of its high water usage – even if it does conjure up nostalgic childhood memories of running through the spray on hot summer days. May even be banned in your area, or in times of drought.

THE RIGHT WAY TO DIG

To avoid backache, make sure the handle of your spade or fork is right for your height, and keep your back straight as you dig.

When I go into the garden with a spade, and dig a bed, I feel such an exhilaration and health that I discover that I have been defrauding myself all this time in letting others do for me what I should have done with my own hands.
RALPH WALDO EMERSON

SAFETY FIRST

Ensure that electrical tools are fitted with a residual current device, or a circuit-breaker, that cuts the supply the second there is power leakage.

KEEP THEM SEPARATE

If you do have to mix up a liquid weedkiller, be sure you apply it in a different watering can from the one you normally use for watering. Labelling it will save confusion – and unnecessary plant death!

<><><><><><><><><><><><><><><><><><><><><><><><><><><><><><><><><><><><><><><><><>

You can bury a lot of troubles digging in the dirt.
ANONYMOUS

<><><><><><><><><><><><><><><><><><><><><><><><><><><><><><><><><><><><><><><><><>

GREEN FINGERS

When weeding, wear an old pair of gloves with the fingers cut off just above the joint. These will protect your hands but still allow your fingers the freedom to do more delicate tasks.

CLEAN NAILS

Try as you might, you can't avoid getting some soil under your nails when gardening. Before you begin, push some soft soap under your nails; it will then be much easier to wash away any embedded soil afterwards.

SOOTHE THOSE BITES

Insect bites are an occupational hazard for the gardener, especially on warm summer evenings when biting insects are on the prowl. An instant, old-fashioned remedy is to squeeze a marigold (Calendula) leaf and rub it on the affected part. This should quickly relieve swelling and itching.

KNEES UP!

Swanky gardening catalogues offers special kneeling pads to protect your knees when planting out or weeding. For a cheaper option, use an old hot-water bottle instead.

TOOL CARE

- Keep an oily rag in the garden shed and wipe tools with it after use, especially on damp days.

- Don't rest spades, hoes and forks on their blades. Hang them to keep them sharp.

- Clean and dry your lawnmower after every use, removing any blades of grass that have been caught in the machinery, then oil the blades – but remember to turn the power off first! Be sure to have the blades sharpened, re-set and oiled after you have used the mower for the last time in autumn, ready for use the next spring.

GET ORGANIZED

A tidy, well-organized tool or potting shed will add to the pleasure of gardening. Try the following tips for keeping down the chaos:

- A narrow band of leather, or old belt or strap, nailed at intervals on the shed wall, makes a handy rack for hanging small tools.

- Save glass jars for storing smaller gardening items – ties, nails, hooks, labels, etc. They'll be easy to find and you'll be able to see when stocks are running low.

- Don't throw away broken pots or crockery. Smash them into smaller pieces and store the pieces, sorted by size, in containers. When needed, use for drainage at the bottom of plant pots.

- Seed, potting and garden composts are sold in bags which can become unwieldy once opened. If you haven't used up all the contents in one go, store the remainder in old buckets or other suitable containers. It will be much easier to lift out with a trowel or spade when needed.

BRIGHT IDEAS

Reinvent ways to use unwanted domestic items by putting them to use in the shed.

- Store small garden items – trowels, forks, secateurs and the like – in an old kitchen vegetable rack. Not only will they be easier to find, but the holes in the rack will allow any dirt to fall through.

- Don't throw away a bristly old doormat. Instead, hang it up on the shed wall and scrape tools on it after use to remove excess soil.

GOING TO SEED

The cheapest way to raise plants is from seed. After all, this is how Nature propagates plants. If you are a novice, it's best to stick to the seeds of hardy annuals – or at the most, half-hardy annuals – and leave biennials, perennials and the rest to more experienced gardeners (until, of course, you become one yourself).

SEEDS FOR FREE

Seed producers constantly tempt us with new varieties of flowering plants, sold in little packets with pictures of immaculate blooms on the front. Although buying these seeds is still cheaper than purchasing the nursery-grown plants, it is possible to get seeds for absolutely nothing – if you do it Nature's way.

Self-sowers

Flowering plants have only one thing in mind – to reproduce and live for eternity! They grow flowers to tempt pollinating insects, which fertilize them and enable them to produce seed. When the flowers fall, the seed-bearing pods are exposed. They ripen and burst, scattering the seed, and *voilà* – a whole new generation of plants is born.

This clever process is known as 'self-sowing' and some plants – such as nasturtiums, euphorbias, aquilegias and fennel – are especially good at it and will need absolutely no encouragement from you. In fact, you'll probably spot some of their babies, self-sown and sprouting, in the most unlikely, far-flung spots – they can even become a nuisance. If you don't want them there, all you'll have to do is either dig up the seedlings and give them to friends or discard them, or transplant them to a more suitable site.

Saving seeds

Other plants may need a little more help, and this is where you come in. During the flowering season, make regular inspections of your garden, with your gardener's notebook and some coloured wool in hand. Tie wool around any plant that is worth saving for seed, and make a note of it. Cut off all but one or two flowering heads (leaving too many seed pods to ripen will put a strain on the plant).

You'll know when the seed is ripe and ready to harvest, because the seed-heads will have become brown and dry – usually in late summer and autumn. Choose a dry and preferably sunny day for collecting so that the seeds are as dry as possible. You can gather the seeds in one of two ways:

1 Place small bags or envelopes over the seed-heads and shake to collect the seeds.

or

2 Cut off the whole seed-head and drop it into the bag. Don't snap it off as this could scatter the seeds you are trying to save. This second method is more effective because all the seeds will fall into the bag. You can discard the pods later.

Don't forget to seal the bags, label and date them. Store in a cool, dry place and sow the following year for a beautiful display of flowers.

SOWING IN TRAYS

You may decide to sow your seed in trays, perhaps because it's still too cold to sow directly outside and you want to give your plants an early start, or because you still need to clear a space for them in the garden. For best results, bear the following in mind:

The importance of hygiene
Whatever container you use for sowing seeds in, make sure it is scrupulously clean by scrubbing it out well first. Good hygiene is essential to prevent damping off, a disease that causes young seedlings to wilt and die.

Watering seedlings
Even though we are all becoming more water-conscious, this is one time not to use the water you've saved in your water butt or barrel. To minimize the risk to young seedlings of damping off disease, water them with mains water instead.

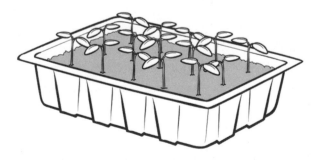

The window sill nursery
If you don't have a greenhouse in which to grow your seedlings, try growing them on a window sill instead. Turn them regularly so they get an equal amount of light.

One for the rook, one for the crow, one to rot,
and one to grow.
TRADITIONAL GARDENER'S SAYING WHEN PLANTING
CORN, BEANS OR PEAS.

In situ

Sowing directly into the soil does mean that you won't have to worry about that fiddly transplanting.

Snug as a bug . . .

In cooler climates, the soil can be too wet and cold early in the season for sowing seeds. You can either wait a couple of weeks until things warm up naturally or, if the soil is reasonably dry, cover it with a couple of layers of horticultural fleece, which will still let moisture through and allow the soil to 'breathe', while warming it up sufficiently for you to get ahead and sow.

All the flowers of all the tomorrows are in the seeds of today.
INDIAN PROVERB

Military precision

No, it's not what happens on the military parade ground – a drill, in gardener speak, is the little trench into which you sow seeds. Vegetables look particularly good grown this way, in straight rows. So, if you want an immaculate plot with rows of veg that would make grandpa proud, place two short canes or stakes at either end of the plot and tie a length of string between them. Drag the edge of a rake or small spade across the soil, using the string as your guide. The result? A perfectly straight little trench. Pop your seeds in, flip the dislodged earth back over the trench, firm gently, water – and wait for the seedlings to emerge.

HOW TO SOW FINE SEEDS

For successful germination, seeds need air, warmth and moisture. If they are sown too deeply, they will be suffocated; if too thickly, the seedlings will choke each other. Getting it right can be particularly tricky with some of the finer seeds – for example, those of poppies – and you can end up sowing a whole clump in one spot.

Sun, sand and seed
For very fine seeds, use an old gardener's trick and mix them with some fine sand – it will then be much easier to sow them evenly.

Top Tip

If birds are a problem in your garden, spread netting over the seedbed to prevent them eating the seed. Alternatively, lay a criss-cross network of light twigs to create a bird barrier.

Top Tip

Always keep a few seeds in reserve in case some of your seedlings don't make it, because of disease, a slug or snail attack or a trampling child or pet.

Sticky fingers
Tip the seeds into your palm, then dampen the index finger of your other hand and use it to pick up a few seeds at a time, which you can then sprinkle on the soil.

DON'T BE FOOLED . . .

All seedlings start off with 'baby leaves' or seed leaves, correctly known as cotyledons. These do not resemble the plant's own distinctive adult leaves, which will be next to appear. So when some ordinary little leaves appear above the soil, don't immediately assume they're weeds – wait to see their second leaves before yanking them out.

DEADHEADING

All a flowering plant wants to do is produce seed, remember? Trick it into producing more flowers by 'deadheading' – removing the dead blooms, along with their seed-pods. Do this regularly and you'll keep your plants flowering for longer.

THE SENSUAL GARDEN

||||||||||||||||||||||||||||||||||||||||||||||||||||||||||||||||||||||||||||||||||||||||||||||||||

There is more to a garden than colour and shape. Include sound and scent, too, for a truly sensual experience.

It is a golden maxim to cultivate the garden for the nose, and the eyes will take care of themselves.
ROBERT LOUIS STEVENSON

SNIFF THIS OUT!

Floral fragrance comes from the volatile oils that plants contain and is one of the methods they use to attract pollinating insects (colour is another) – it just so happens that we humans also appreciate their beautiful perfume. There are two main types of fragrant plant: those with scented flowers and those with aromatic leaves.

- Plants with scented leaves are fragrant all season as long as they are in leaf, but give off their perfume most powerfully when touched, so put them somewhere where you are likely to brush against them often.

- Plants with scented flowers release their perfume directly into the air, but obviously are only perfumed when in flower.

Grow them close to the patio, or anywhere that you frequent. There's no point in tucking them away in some far corner that you hardly ever visit. Some flowers are only fragrant at night. These are especially good to have near a seating area so you can enjoy their perfume while sipping a nice glass of chilled wine at the end of the day.

CHEAT'S PERFUME

If you have people coming over for dinner and have fantasies of eating al fresco in a perfumed haven but have no scented plants, here's how to cheat. Just before your guests arrive, spray some nearby flowers with a few drops of essential oil diluted in a little water. They'll never know!

◇◇

We can complain because rose bushes have thorns, or rejoice because thorn bushes have roses.
ABRAHAM LINCOLN

◇◇

ONLY A ROSE

Roses are the ultimate scented plants. If perfume is top of your agenda, make sure you choose the most fragrant varieties – some modern roses have been bred for looks rather than perfume. A word of warning though: don't plant new roses in a bed where other roses have been grown for two years or more, or they will almost certainly succumb to 'rose sickness' and may even die. This soil-borne condition is thought to be due to harmful pests and diseases that have built up over the years around the roots of the old plants, and are now concentrated in this one area.

GROW A SCENTED LAWN

Plant a patch of non-flowering camomile, the kind sold for making camomile lawns. When you walk over it, the pressure of your feet will release its perfume. However, this kind of lawn is not for everyday use: you won't be able to walk on it frequently or let the kids and dog loose on it, as you could with ordinary grass. A camomile lawn is therefore best in a secluded corner or some area specially set aside for the purpose.

GROW A PERFUMED PATH

If you don't want to go the whole hog and spend money on plants for a scented lawn, try a perfumed path instead. You can use camomile or any other low-growing aromatic herb. Make sure the soil is well drained. Dig in plenty of grit – about 2 bucketfuls of the stuff per square metre. Level the soil, spread with a thick layer of gravel, then get planting. Space your herbs about 15 cm (6 in) apart. If you need to use the path a lot, add stepping stones to walk on – you'll still step on some of the herbs as you go, releasing their scent.

STEP ON THE CRACKS!

Sow the seeds of low-growing scented herbs into the cracks between paving stones.

MAKE A HERB SEAT

For this you will need:

square wooden tub (the kind sold for patios)
trellis for the back of the seat
crocks for drainage
potting compost
low-growing, tough aromatic herbs,
such as thyme, rosemary or camomile

1 Attach the trellis to the back of the tub, to form the back of the seat. Place it where you want the finished seat to go as it can be quite heavy when filled.

2 If necessary, raise the tub on some bricks or a wooden stand (treated to make it weatherproof) so that the top will be a convenient height for sitting on.

3 Fill the bottom of the tub with crocks, then top up with compost, plant your herbs and water them in. Allow them to become established before sitting on them. If you can't bear the idea of squashing them, just press them with your hand when passing to release their scent.

Variation Make a herb bench with two tubs and some planks of wood for a seat.

><<<<<<<<<<<<<<<<<<<<<<<<<<<<<<<<<<<<<<<<<<<<<<<<<<<<<<<<<<<<<<<<<<<

So will I build my altar in the fields,
And the blue sky my fretted dome shall be,
And the sweet fragrance that the wild flower yields
Shall be the incense I will yield to thee.
SAMUEL TAYLOR COLERIDGE

><<<<<<<<<<<<<<<<<<<<<<<<<<<<<<<<<<<<<<<<<<<<<<<<<<<<<<<<<<<<<<<<<<<

PERFUMED POND

Grow scented plants near your garden pond. On warm days, the humid air will intensify their perfume.

THE SOUND CREW

Often the forgotten element in gardens, sound can add a whole extra sensory dimension to the experience. Think about:

- Moving water. You may not have space for a babbling brook, but even the smallest garden can accommodate a fountain of some sort, for that gently trickling sound.

- Wind chimes. Metal ones tinkle; bamboo makes more of a satisfying clunk. Choose whichever produces the sound effect you like best.

- Rustling plants. Grasses and bamboos are great if you want the rustle factor.

- Birdsong and humming bees. Encourage wildlife to your garden and you will get natural sound effects for free.

THE DRY GARDEN

With the growing concern over global warming, we all need to use the Earth's resources responsibly, and that includes water. In the garden, that means three things: water with care; use water conservation methods; and grow plants that are tolerant of drought.

DROUGHT-TOLERANT PLANTS

If you live in a dry area or are concerned about water conservation, you may have to give up fantasies of a cottage garden or lush green swathes of lawn – but there is no need to despair. It is simply a matter of changing your style and choosing plants that tolerate – or even like – dry conditions. The range is so vast you will be spoilt for choice, and includes herbs such as lavender through to poppies, the architectural euphorbias and sedums, the magnificent *crambe cordifolia* with its foaming cascade of white flowers, ornamental grasses, maritime plants such as sea hollies, and even trees such as holly. Many of these plants have striking shapes as well as brightly coloured flowers, so take advice from your local garden centre or consult a good illustrated gardening book.

GIVE THEM SHELTER

Erect a windbreak around plants to protect them from the drying effects of wind. This could be a hardy hedge or some kind of fencing.

ALL SPACED OUT

In drier areas, space plants slightly wider apart than usually required to give the roots a larger area to 'drink' from.

WATER, WATER EVERYWHERE

Watering your plants is not just a matter of spraying them with the hose briefly in the evening. Here are the dos and don'ts of giving your garden a drink.

Less is more
It is better to water heavily and less frequently than lightly and more often. Soaking the soil encourages the roots to delve deep, and a deep root system enables plants to withstand drought better. Shallow watering, on the other hand, encourages shallow, surface rooting.

When often is best
The exception to the above rule concerns young plants – water them frequently and lightly so that they never dry out.

Watch where you go!
Direct the water to the base of each plant.

Waste not, want not
Keep the weeds down! That way none of that precious water will be wasted on them, and will go only where you want it to go – to your prized plants.

GET MULCHING

A mulch is a thick layer of material, preferably 10–15 cm (4–6 in) deep, around a plant. It may be made up of organic material, such as bark chippings or compost, or inorganic material such as coarse grit or gravel. Mulches serve several functions: they can enrich the soil and improve its texture, and they can reduce water loss from the soil. For most plants of small to medium size spread the mulch loosely over an area that matches the spread of the foliage canopy but keep the main stem of the plant clear.

Remember, too, that a mulch is an insulator, so what it keeps in, stays in. That means that if you lay it over a cold, water-logged soil, the soil is more likely to stay that way, so you should wait till it has dried out a little and the weather has warmed. Alternatively, if you mulch over a dry soil, this will reduce the amount of water getting through so water well first. Also take care to remove all perennial weeds beforehand or they will reap the benefits intended for your plants!

When deciding on a mulch, consider the following:

COARSE BARK

✓ Long-lasting and does not mix in with soil as quickly as other organic mulches

✓ Cannot be dislodged by rain, and loose structure allows rain to pass through

✓ Prevents weed seeds from germinating (and weeds steal water from your plants); any weeds that do come through can easily be removed

✓ May improve texture of soil

✗ Does not add nutrients to soil

GARDEN COMPOST

✓ Improves texture of soil; adds nutrients

✓ Allows rain to pass through (though not as well as bark)

✗ Does not last as long as bark because it mixes in with the soil over time

✗ Provides an ideal growing medium for weeds

COARSE GRIT AND GRAVEL

✓ Very long-lasting

✓ Allow rain to pass through without reducing moisture loss

✗ Do not enrich the soil

SAVE WATER

Wherever we live, we are all becoming increasingly aware of the preciousness of the Earth's resources and water is one of the most precious of all.

Water butt

To conserve as much water as possible, why not set up a water butt? Connected via a downpipe to the guttering, this reroutes the rainwater that falls on your roof into the butt, rather than letting it run away into the drains. You can then fill a watering can from the tap at the bottom. You may need to raise the butt on a special stand or some bricks, so there is space to fit the can below the tap. Rainwater is perfect for acid-loving plants that don't like the alkalinity of mains water. Check out the different types of butt available at your DIY store and ask for advice on the best one for your needs.

Don't waste a drop!

Once cool, water from boiling or steaming food can be used on plants, as can the first two fillings of a drinking water filter. Even bathwater, provided it doesn't have too many products in it, can be recycled to give your garden a drink. Think before you pour it away: can I use this for watering?

THE NO-LAWN GARDEN

Lush lawns need a lot of watering to get that velvety green look. Gravel or paving, on the other hand, require neither watering nor cutting. So give the Earth and yourself a break, and go for a no-lawn garden. There are many types of gravel and paving available, all of which can contribute greatly to the style and design of your plot.

DRY GARDEN STYLES

- Go for a Mediterranean-style garden with a fig tree, perhaps an oleander or two, some drought-tolerant perennials and grasses, some plants in big pots – and a seat in the shade of the fig tree where you can sit and relax. In warmer climes, you could also try bougainvillea with its red or cerise flowers. The epitome of the hot, dry Mediterranean garden, this climber will clamber up walls and cover them with a stunning display of colour.

- Cacti and succulents are the ultimate drought-tolerant plants, naturally adapted to life in the driest of climates. They have amazing architectural forms and some produce beautiful flowers too. Combined with grasses and gravel, they'll make a stunning display – but they do need heat.

POT LUCK

A few hours spent in a garden centre drooling over the wonderful items for sale can lead to serious temptation, and leave your pockets a lot lighter at the end of your visit – thus are we seduced into parting with our cash by visions of instant gardens with minimum effort. But don't let lack of lolly hold you back. Be like the canny old-time gardeners and grow your own plants from seeds and cuttings (*see pages 24-9 and 56-9*) and get inventive with cheap or even free containers.

RECYCLE, RECLAIM, REUSE

- Why buy special pots for growing seedlings when you can recycle containers from the kitchen for free? It'll save you money and save on waste too. When they are empty, wash out plastic food containers such as yogurt pots, ice cream tubs, egg boxes, takeaway curry containers, etc., then make holes in the bottom for drainage. If the container is made of plastic, the bottom may split if you try to pierce it. Instead, heat a metal skewer over a flame and carefully melt a few holes in the plastic. Larger food trays make serviceable seed trays. Pierce holes in the base and cover loosely with clingfilm or a clear polythene bag to keep seedlings warm as they emerge. Remove the covering when the weather is warmer.

- Save large plastic drinks bottles, cut in half and use the tops as cloches to protect seedlings growing in the open ground. Not only will they keep the seedlings warm but they'll also give protection against marauding slugs and snails that like nothing better than juicy young foliage.

HOLD IT!

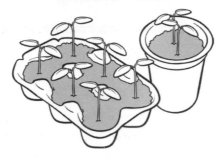

Almost any container that is rigid enough and made of material that won't rot can be pressed into service as a plant container. Drill drainage holes in the bottom, add pieces of broken pottery to aid drainage, fill with compost, and you're away. If the container is made of metal, bear in mind that this will heat up more than other materials, so site in a cooler position, or grow your plant in a smaller pot that you can place inside the metal one. Give jaded-looking containers a new lease of life by applying a coat of paint to the outside, in a colour that will complement the plant you are growing. For a great visual effect, arrange your containers together with the tallest at the back. Try these ideas:

- Rigid builders' buckets, available from hardware and DIY stores, are cheap and durable.

- Stacking storage boxes, no longer needed for storing things, can be recycled as elegant plant containers.

- Galvanized buckets can bring a rustic look to your garden style.

- Old paint pots in 1-litre, 2.5-litre or 5-litre sizes, thoroughly cleaned inside, have the fashionable straight-sided shape that suits modern garden design. Paint the outsides and arrange in groups of the same or different sizes.

Top Tip

Even if you are looking for freebies or cheapies and so won't have that much choice, consider your container size, shape and style in relation to the plants it will contain. Go for dramatic contrast: for example, rustic wicker with architectural plants, or straight-sided paint pots with a mass of bright flowers.

- Wicker baskets, lined with polythene (don't forget the drainage holes at the bottom), make delightful cottage-style plant containers. If they are going to stand out in the open, protect the bases from damp by placing them on a brick to lift them off the paving.

- Refuse bins now come in various sizes and finishes. The traditional black plastic ones have a utilitarian feel, but the metal and enamelled types can look very decorative. Depending on their size they can be very deep, however, so unless you want to grow something that requires a depth of soil – such as potatoes – you can 'cheat' by half-filling with broken bricks, stones, broken polystyrene packaging, then top up with soil. Or, as with galvanized buckets, grow your plant in a smaller container that you can place inside, propped up to achieve the correct height.

MOVE IT!

Make heavier plant pots easier to move by placing them on wheeled stands. You can buy these from gardening catalogues or make your own. Use a square of decking, cut to size if necessary, and attach strong castors to the base.

IN THE GUTTER

If you want to grow salad crops in rows, a convenient way of getting them started is to sow the seeds in a length of guttering. Peas can also be sown this way.

1. Cut some guttering to length: it should be no more than about 60 cm (2 ft) long for ease of handling.
2. Fill it with peat-free compost, stopping just short of the ends and pressing it down firmly so that it is level with the top.
3. Sow the seeds in the compost, spacing them evenly along the guttering. If sowing early in the year in colder climates, keep them in an unheated greenhouse.
4. When the seedlings are ready to plant out, dig a shallow trench in the soil the same length and depth as the guttering. Carefully lower the guttering into it to test it for size, without disturbing the seedlings.
5. Now for the fun part. Gently slide the whole row of seedlings into the trench and – hey presto! – instant vegetable garden!

WHERE THERE'S MUCK

|||||||||||||||||||||||||||||||||||||||||||||||||||||||||||||||||||||||||||||||||||||||||||||||

The soil is where it all begins. It is the medium in which your plants are rooted, and which determines much of their health.

N P P – THE THREE ESSENTIALS

The soil is your plants' larder, and their roots soak up its soluble nutrients through the moisture in the soil – which is why plants need watering. Soil contains three main nutrients that are essential for plant health. A lack of any one of these will show in your plants in different ways.

- **Nitrogen** for leaves and general vigour

- **Potash** for flowers and fruit

- **Phosphorus** for strong roots

A nitrogen deficiency will lead to reduced growth, while leaf discoloration is a sign of potash deficiency.

Ashes to ashes
If you have real log fires, don't bin the ashes and soot: sprinkle them around your plants. They contain potash.

THE SOIL IN WINTER

- Avoid digging the soil when it's frozen, as this will destroy its structure.

- Cover any bare ground with hessian-backed carpet or plastic sheeting to deter weeds (*see next page*).

Soil . . . scoop up a handful of the magic stuff. Look at it closely. What wonders it holds as it lies there in your palm. Tiny sharp grains of sand, little faggots of wood and leaf fibre, infinitely small round pieces of marble, fragments of shell, specks of black carbon, a section of vertebrae from some minute creature. And mingling with it all the dust of countless generations of plants and flowers, trees, animals and – yes – our own, age-long forgotten forebears, gardeners of long ago. Can this incredible composition be the common soil?

FROM *THE SEASONS THROUGH*
BY STUART MADDOX MASTERS

THE BIG COVER-UP

What do you do with an old carpet after you've had new carpet laid? Use it in the garden! Covering bare ground with carpet in winter will make your job as a gardener that much easier. First of all, for those of us in cooler climes, it will keep the soil warmer and more workable. Second, it's a great way to smother weeds – without light, many of them simply give up.

- Hessian-backed stair carpet is ideal as this comes in convenient strips. Avoid foam-backed nylon carpets as these will disintegrate.

- Black plastic sheeting is another alternative. It should preferably be the special type from garden centres as this is porous and allows moisture through – ordinary black plastic will need to have slits cut in it to allow the rain through, and won't last as long.

- Flattened cardboard boxes, weighed down with stones and bricks, is another, if rather unsightly, option.

THE SOIL IN SPRING

In spring, lightly fork around plants and bulbs in the herbaceous border to aerate the soil and give the plants a head start in their growth.

Pelleted chicken manure is a useful fertilizer that can be applied to your soil in spring. It's easy to handle too.

THE SOIL IN SUMMER

Apply a fertilizer that is high in potash, such as tomato food, to encourage fruiting plants to crop.

For faster results, feed plants with a liquid fertilizer, applied to the roots or sprayed on the leaves.

Man – despite his artistic pretensions, his sophistication, and his many accomplishments – owes his existence to a six-inch layer of topsoil and the fact that it rains.

ANONYMOUS

THE SOIL IN AUTUMN

- A thick layer of organic matter, such as well-rotted manure, 8–10 cm (3–4 in) deep, spread over the soil in autumn, will help to maintain the soil's fertility. This is especially true for lighter soils whose nutrients are more easily washed out by rain.

- Beneath the seemingly inert surface of the soil there's a whole army of wriggly helpers – earthworms! When you spread manure on the earth, you don't need to bother to dig it in: the worms will slowly work it in for you.

FOR PEAT'S SAKE!

Peat bogs are important wildlife habitats, formed over hundreds of years, and the extraction of peat for use in gardening has contributed hugely to their destruction. Peat can become waterlogged and, if it dries out, it can be hard to get it to hold moisture again so, for environmental as well as practical reasons, go for one of the many peat-free alternatives instead.

MAKE YOUR OWN COMPOST

Composting is a great way to recycle kitchen and garden waste. Once it has rotted down, you can dig it into the soil to improve its structure, or use it as a mulch. You can buy compost bins or make your own from pallets or old floorboards. As the organic matter decays, heat is produced that speeds the process of turning those veg peelings and garden trimmings into a lovely, crumbly, sweet-smelling compost. The contents of your heap must be turned to aerate them and to expose them to the higher temperatures in the middle. If your container doesn't have a lid, cover it with a piece of old carpet to keep the rain out and the heat in.

Don't treat your compost heap as a kind of trash can and add any old refuse to it.

Say yes to:

- ✓ small annual weeds
- ✓ the tops of perennial weeds (not the roots)
- ✓ grass cuttings, mixed in so they don't make a slimy mess
- ✓ young hedge clippings
- ✓ wood ash from the fireplace

✓ raw vegetable and fruit peelings
✓ chopped raw vegetables or fruit
✓ cardboard

Remember to chop up any thicker or more woody stems.

Say no to:

✗ cooked food and meat as these can attract rats
✗ the roots of tough perennial weeds: if these don't rot down they'll resprout
✗ plants that have been infected with any fungal disease; the spores will remain in the compost, ready to re-infect other plants when you spread it on the soil the following year
✗ newspapers and glossy magazines, as they do not compost well
✗ coal ash from the fireplace
✗ dog and cat faeces

Top Tip

Keep a small, easy-to-move lidded bin by the kitchen door and pop your kitchen peelings into it as you go.

GOING UP?

Taller plants bring structural interest to a border, while climbers, with their vertical growth, are great plants to go for if you want a beautiful display but are short of space. As well as clothing walls and fences with decorative flowers, they are also useful if you want to disguise an eyesore, such as an ugly shed or fence.

SHAPE UP

Everybody needs a bit of support now and then, and that applies to plants as much as humans. Many flowering plants require help so they don't flop over into a shapeless heap as they grow.

- Supports for bushy perennials should be put in place early in spring. Specially designed supports, consisting of plastic-coated grids on legs, are available in various sizes. For a cheaper, improvised option, use squares of wide-mesh wire. Place the supports over the shoots and allow them to grow up through the squares. As they grow, gently pull up the supports. If using wire, a stake slipped through the netting when the plant is about 23 cm (9 in) high, and driven into the ground, will give added support.

- Strong-growing perennials need one or two short stakes with a strand of wire looped around the plants and fastened to the stake. As they grow, loop another wire circle around the plant and attach to the same stake higher up.

- Dahlias need strong stakes put in place when the tubers are planted.

- Twigs and pea sticks are inconspicuous and are good for supporting plants of soft, sappy growth, such as sweet peas.

- Tie up tall annuals with green twist or soft twine, and fasten to a strong bamboo cane or stick.

TYING THE KNOT

You can tie plants to their supports with plastic-coated wire ties, or with garden string. If using string, tie it in a neat figure-of-eight, with one of the loops wrapped and knotted firmly but gently around the stem and the other, larger loop attached to the cane or stake. That way, there will be less friction on the stem when the plant moves in the breeze, as the string won't pull against the stem and cut into it.

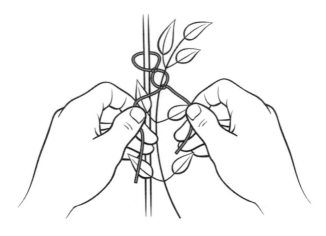

CANE CARE

- So you don't blind yourself by poking yourself in the eye on a bamboo cane, cover the ends of canes with small, up-ended, plastic drinks bottles.

- When the flowering period is over, collect all stakes and canes, wash them, tie up in bundles and store in the shed for use again next year.

FOR THE RECORD

- In 2005, a rose belonging to Paul and Sharon Palumbo, of San Diego, California, reached a record height, as the tallest self-supported rose bush, of 4.03 m (13^1/4 ft).

- In 1971, G.E. Hooking of Kington Langley, Wiltshire, England, grew a record sunflower which reached 5.05 m (16 ft 2 in) in height. In 1976, Frank Killand, of Exeter, England, bettered this achievement with his 7-m (23^1/2-ft) tall sunflower. In 2002, Melvin Hemker of Saint Charles, Michigan, was awarded the Guinness World Record for sunflowers which grew to a tiddly 3.6 m (12 ft) or so.

HOLD ON

Climbers? You've got to hand it to them! They have such inventive ways of reaching for the sky. Most need permanent support by way of trellis or wire, and some will need tying in too.

- The 'stickers' either have aerial roots, such as ivy, or adhesive tips on their tendrils, such as Virginia creeper. This means they are self-clinging and won't need help to climb except in the early stages – they can also pull mortar out of brickwork so best to keep them off house walls!

- The 'twiners', such as honeysuckle or wisteria, coil themselves clockwise or anticlockwise around their supports.

- The 'curlers', such as trailing nasturtiums or clematis, attach themselves by means of curling leaf stalks.

- The 'sensitives' cling on with their touch-sensitive tendrils.

- The 'hookers' have hooked thorns, which they use to hook onto their host plants. If not scrambling though other plants, they'll need tying to sturdy supports.

- The 'slackers', such as bougainvillea, attach only loosely and need all the help they can get.

HANG IT UP

How do you get to a wall or fence to paint it or treat with wood preservative when the whole thing is smothered in your favourite climber? Easy! Grow the plant on a movable trellis. Instead of fixing the trellis in place with screws, just hang it on hooks instead. When it comes to repainting, carefully lift off the whole thing – trellis and climber – and lay it on the ground, covered with a dustsheet, while you work. When you're done, just hang it back up again. Easy peasy.

WHAT A BRICK!

Brick walls in a sunny spot act like storage heaters, retaining and radiating warmth when the day is done. This 'central heating' effect means that, in cooler, temperate climates, you can grow more tender climbers against a brick wall than you could in more exposed sites. A wall can also give some frost protection.

EDIBLE CLIMBERS

Trailing fruit and vegetables can be incredibly decorative, so instead of flowers why not grow an edible climber up your fence or wall? Try melons, members of the squash and pumpkin family, or cucumbers. Not only will you get lush leaves and flowers, you'll get food too! What could be nicer?

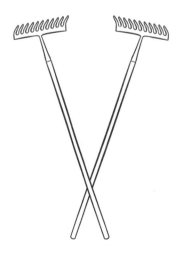

CUTTING EDGE

Isn't Nature wonderful? If you know how to work with her, she'll give you plants for free. Taking cuttings from perennial plants, or dividing them, is the way to go.

PROPAGATE A PELARGONIUM

Pelargonium? That's the posh (and correct) name for geranium. Everyone loves geraniums. The red ones especially are evocative of whitewashed Mediterranean houses, where pots and window-boxes of bright flowers add an extra splash of colour. Their leaves are scented too. Here's how to get more:

1. Fill a small pot with peat-free all-purpose compost.
2. Using secateurs, cut a 15-cm (6-in) shoot from a healthy geranium plant. Make the cut just below a leaf joint – that's the bumpy bit where the leaf stalk joins the main stem.

3. Remove the lower leaves and any flowers or buds from the shoot.

④ Make a hole in the centre of the compost with a pencil and insert the cutting. Tap the pot gently to firm the compost. Water lightly, and cover with a clear plastic bag, secured with a rubber band, to keep the cutting in a humid atmosphere and prevent drying out. Water the cutting again only if it wilts. In a few weeks, it should have rooted. You can grow several cuttings in one pot.

You can use the same technique with green cuttings from other perennials and shrubs.

DIVIDE AND MULTIPLY

To get more of the same perennial without spending any extra money, divide it. Simply dig up the parent plant with a fork and separate it into two or more clumps, each with its own roots and leaves, and replant.

Top Tips

- *To prevent your cuttings drying out while you are collecting them, place them in a plastic bag, add a few drops of water and shake to keep them moist and stop them wilting.*

- *Make sure you grow several cuttings from each plant, in case one or two fail to root.*

- *Most cuttings root better if the cut end is first dipped in hormone rooting powder or liquid.*

- You can divide some plants just by gently pulling the root ball apart.

- For others, insert two garden forks back to back in the centre of the clump and lever it apart.

- Alternatively, cut through the clump with a pruning saw or bread knife.

Replant the divisions as soon as possible and keep the new plants well watered until they are established.

*If, instead of talking to your plants,
you yelled at them, would they still grow,
only to be troubled and insecure?*

GO FORTH AND MULTIPLY

Some plants need no encouragement to propagate themselves, dropping their seeds all over the place. Keep an eye open for these self-sown seedlings. If you spot some you want to keep, label them and then, in the autumn, move them to their final position or pot them up until you are ready to plant them out. A word of warning though – it's best not to let them get too big before you lift them, or you could have a heavy digging job on your hands.

Top Tip

In spring, when you're buying perennial plants at the garden centre, look out for any that are large and have filled their pots. When you get them home you may be able to divide them before planting them out, and get two – or more – plants for the price of one.

WEED IT OUT

It may be pressure of time or changing tastes, but gardeners are no longer so obsessed with getting rid of every weed in sight. After all, as native flora, weeds have more of a right to be there than those tender, exotic imports, and their leaves and flowers provide just the food that native fauna want. Some can even look quite pretty! So develop a more relaxed attitude to weeds and keep them under control rather than try the impossible – to eradicate them completely. And even if you are not particularly 'green', there is no need to use weedkiller. There are other, gentler, ways of dealing with the problem.

LITTLE AND OFTEN

It's simple – if you want to keep down weeds, remove them little and often. Pottering about, hand-weeding, can even be quite a pleasurable experience.

- Annual weeds can go on the compost heap.

- Persistent perennial weeds need to be binned: even the tiniest bit of root can regrow. Be as persistent in removing them as they are in growing, and you can at least keep them under control.

HOE WONDERFUL!

One of the easiest ways to keep down weeds is with a hoe. Hold the blade of the hoe level with the top of the soil and slide it along to slice through the stems of the weeds. Even the most persistent ones such as bindweed can be kept in check this way. All plants depend on their leaves to photosynthesize, a complex process that is the ultimate solar power. Using the chlorophyll (green colouring) in their leaves, plants trap the energy from the sun to produce sugar. Remove the leaves and you remove these little powerhouses of growth. But you will need to hoe little and often so that the weeds don't get out of hand. And take care not to get over-enthusiastic or you may slice through the stem of one of your prized plants.

When weeding, the best way to make sure you are removing a weed and not a valuable plant is to pull on it. If it comes out of the ground easily, it is a valuable plant.

ANONYMOUS

WEED-FREE FLOWER BEDS

- Suppress weeds in the flower bed by planting densely so they don't get a look in.

- Use a mulch, such as bark chippings, leaf mould or gravel, to smother weeds. It should be no less than 10 cm (4 in) deep, and applied to the soil only after all the weeds have been removed.

- To clear a large area of weeds, lay down a light-excluding membrane, such as black polythene. Special sheeting is available at DIY stores and garden centres.

WEED-FREE PATHS AND SEATING AREAS

- When spreading gravel on a path, lay down a special permeable membrane underneath to smother any weeds that might otherwise rear their heads through the gravel.

- Point paving stones with mortar rather than sand, which would provide a growing medium for weeds. Once they have rooted in the cracks between paving, they can be extremely hard to remove.

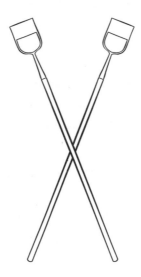

BE YOUR OWN
PLANT DOCTOR

Just like us humans, plants suffer from a range of ailments brought on by various plant parasites, whether they be leaf-eating insects or creeping fungal diseases. In the case of the former, what we label 'pests' are just wild creatures that come uninvited into our gardens trying to eke out a living! Sometimes, though, they invite all their relations along too and things get out of hand. That's when you need to take action.

GET THE PICTURE

A picture is worth a thousand words, they say, so arm yourself with a good illustrated gardening book showing pictures of beneficial insects and garden predators and, if possible, the damage they do. For example, lily beetles – the ones that eat their way through the leaves of your prize lilies – are coloured bright red, and can easily be mistaken for beneficial aphid-eating ladybirds. Get the picture, and learn to distinguish friend from foe.

QUICK, QUICK, SLOW

As a very rough rule of thumb, plant-chomping pests are sluggish vegetarians; pest-eating predators are nippy carnivores.

LET NATURE DO IT

It is possible to keep pest numbers under control by collaborating with Nature rather than getting in her way by using pesticides, so make this your first line of attack.

Grow the right plants

Choose insect-attracting plants to entice natural predators into your garden, and let them do their job. Companion planting – growing plants that attract predators next to those that attract their prey, or growing more dispensible plants that are more attractive to pests than the more prized adjacent specimens – is a more sophisticated version of this idea.

Encourage wildlife

Natural balance is what it's all about. Set up bird boxes and bird baths, and grow hedges to encourage birds to your garden. Make a pile of logs to provide shelter for hedgehogs, and invite frogs and other amphibians by creating a small pond. All of these will feast on pests and create a good predator–prey balance. The richer biodiversity will make your garden hum with life, and give you pleasure too.

Bring in the heavy mob

Introduce natural predators yourself, such as nematodes – parasites that prey on plant-eating species – to your garden. Buy whichever species prey on the pest you want to control. Many are available by mail order and come packaged with instructions for use.

DO IT YOURSELF

If Nature isn't quite doing it for you, you can intervene with the following non-chemical methods.

Catch 'em in the act

Tedious it may be, but picking predators off by hand and disposing of them is, in some cases, the best option. Aphids, for example, can simply be rubbed off with your fingers. Lily beetles or vine weevils, which cause damage over a long period and are difficult to control otherwise, can be caught and crushed underfoot: a quick but merciful death.

Spray 'em off

Spraying with water or with a light washing-up liquid solution is a tried and tested method for getting rid of sap-sucking aphids and similar species.

Go organic

Garden centres sell environmentally safe deterrents, based on plant oils and other organic substances, which deter or even kill specific garden pests.

IF ALL ELSE FAILS . . .

With serious infestations, you may have no alternative but to use a pesticide. Remember that these are poisons, so apply with great care and always follow the manufacturer's instructions. There are two main types: contact, which kill on contact with a leaf or other part; and systemic, which are absorbed into the plant's system.

Remember, too, that many other unlikely-sounding products – including hormone rooting powder – are classified as pesticides, and need the same careful handling.

Think of others
Spray at dusk, when the bees have gone to bed, in case the chemicals are harmful to them too. Spray when the air is still, to avoid pesticide drift, and keep away from ponds that may contain fish, amphibians and other aquatic life.

Dispose of safely
Pesticides are classified as hazardous waste, so when you've finished with them:
- ✘ don't pour them down the sink
- ✘ don't put them in the bin unless the label says you can
- ✘ don't put them on a garden bonfire (they can give off poisonous fumes or be too inflammable to burn safely)
- ✓ do consult your local authority about their safe disposal

BE A GOOD GARDENER

Pests are not the only challenge gardeners face. Fungal diseases such as rust or black spot are common, and there may be nutritional deficiencies and other ailments too – your plants will tell you when they're not feeling well. Proper basic practice and hygiene can go a long way to preventing problems and keeping your plants healthy. Here are just a few dos and don'ts:
- ✓ feed plants regularly so they don't suffer from nitrogen, potassium, phosphate, manganese, magnesium or iron

deficiency (yellowed or discoloured leaves, slow growth or early leaf-drop)

✓ ensure that plants receive sufficient water so they do not suffer from drought (premature autumn colour and early leaf-drop)

✓ remove and destroy (do not compost) affected leaves in cases of rust (brown or orange or spots on leaves) or black spot (yellowing leaves with brown and black spots that then wither and drop); regularly spraying susceptible plants, such as roses, with a proprietary fungicide helps too

✓ remove and destroy leaves infected with rust or black spot that have fallen to the ground and keep the area tidy, to limit the spread of the spores

✗ don't water in hot sunlight as water on the leaves can scorch them; water in the evening on dull days

✗ don't apply insecticides or fungicides in hot, sunny weather, or too often or at the wrong dosage, as this can cause the leaves to bleach and scorch

ON THE SLIME TRAIL

Snails and their slug cousins are no friends of the gardener and can demolish treasured garden plants in record time. Traditionally, poisonous pellets were used to kill them but as these can be fatal to pets and wildlife, there are a number of safer alternatives you can try.

ALL TOGETHER NOW!

Place upturned pots or prop up tiles or slates in strategic spots around the garden, or spread plastic bags or sheeting on the ground. Slugs and snails will gather underneath, making it easy to collect and dispose of them.

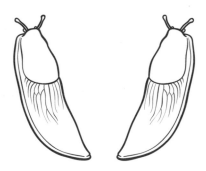

ROUGH IT UP

Make it harder for slugs and snails to slither along their slime trail by applying a coarse mulch around vulnerable plants.

Certain aromas will put them off too. Try the following:

- coffee grounds

- broken egg shells

- sharp sand or grit

- pine needles or oak leaves

- chopped hair (including human hair)

- dry straw or sawdust

- shredded bark, pine bark chips, black peat or cocoa shell mulch

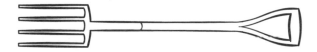

- aromatic herbs such as mint or lemon balm (but these will need frequent replacing)

- dry soot mixed with sharp cinders, or fresh, dry ashes

- cat litter, especially types containing diatomite, a form of marine algae

- orange peel

- cotton wool, tied around individual stems

GREASEPROOF

Smear a thick band of Vaseline around the rim of plant pots: the pests' sticky slime trail will find it harder to adhere to this.

HEAVY METAL

Wrap copper bands or foil around plant pots. Wide copper bands can be placed around beds. Metals such as aluminium are also said to be toxic to slugs.

WILD FRIENDS

Frogs, toads, newts, hedgehogs, birds, centipedes and certain ground beetles all like to feast on these pests, so do whatever you can to encourage them into your garden. Thrushes are especially partial to snails.

MICRO-WARRIORS

Nematodes, available by mail order, are microscopic organisms that are especially effective in dealing with smaller, underground-dwelling slugs. They kill the slugs by laying their eggs in them.

LAGER LOUTS

Fill containers with beer, bury them level with the soil, and leave overnight. Lured by the heady aroma, slugs and snails will climb in and drown, and you can then discard the corpses the following morning. If you think beer is far too good to waste on these pests, keep it for yourself and use a mixture of yeast and water instead.

PICK OF THE BUNCH

Slugs and snails are especially active two to three hours after sunset – if you stand quietly, you may even be able to hear the slurp-slurp as they suck away at your prized plants. They are also active after rain or during damp weather. Keep an eye open and pick off those that you spot. If all else fails, try organic slug pellets which contain ferrous phosphate.

SNAILS IN GARLIC

The French eat them smothered in garlic butter, but you can give snails, and slugs, a taste of garlic while they're still alive – and keep them off your plants at the same time. It seems that slugs and snails don't like its pungent taste.

1. Crush two bulbs of garlic – that's the whole head, not just individual cloves.
2. Blanch them (boil briefly to soften) in 1 litre (2 pints) of water for 3–4 minutes.
3. Strain, and top up the mixture to 1 litre (2 pints) again. Leave to cool.
4. To use, stir 1 tablespoon into 4.5 litres (1 gallon) of water, sprinkle onto the foliage and allow to dry. Apply in dry weather so that rain does not dilute the wash. You'll need to reapply every two weeks.

GREEN AND PLEASANT

|||||||||||||||||||||||||||||||||||||||||||||||||||||||||||||||||||||||||||||||||||||||||||||||||||

Just as a well-made bed instantly makes a room look tidier, so a well-cared-for lawn sets off the rest of the garden. But don't try for perfection – remember that the stripy green-velvet lawn that you lust after is usually the work of a team of professional gardeners.

LAWN SHAPES

- A circular lawn can make a garden feel larger than it really is.

- A long narrow lawn with straight sides will draw the eye to the bottom of the garden, making it seem longer.

- An L-shaped lawn that disappears behind shrubs will bring an air of mystery to the garden, tempting you to explore what's 'round the bend'.

SEED OR TURF?

Turf produces an almost instant lawn with that wonderful, lush greenness that we all love. Seed is cheaper and comes in convenient packages that you can carry through the house without mucking up your carpet. Conveniently, there are different seed mixes for different needs. Fescue and bent grass produce a fine-quality lawn – more for gazing on in admiration than tramping over – while dwarf rye grasses are tougher and better suited to a child-friendly garden.

There are even special mixes for dry sites and light shade under trees. If you want to avoid worn areas in your lawn, lay a path or stepping-stones for walking on instead of the grass.

THE FABULOUS FIVE

To keep your lawn in tip-top condition, you'll need this basic kit:

- Wire-toothed lawn rake, for raking the surface

- Garden fork, for aerating the soil

- Long-handled shears, for trimming the edges

- Daisy grubber, a cunning forked tool for hooking weeds out of the lawn

- Lawnmower, for cutting the lawn – do this regularly to keep grass healthy

- Optional extra: a half-moon edger for annual cutting of untidy, overgrown edges

WATERING

If you have to water, water the lawn once the soil becomes dry, but before the grass colour changes. If the ground is very hard, aerating before watering can aid water penetration. Watering once a week to ten days is normally sufficient. Ensure that the water reaches a depth of 10 cm (4 in); in the middle of summer 1 sq m will need 20 litres (4 gallons) every seven days.

In dry weather, raise the height of cut to avoid weakening the grasses. Letting the clippings fall back onto the lawn during dry spells can slow down the evaporation of water from the soil surface. But you must make sure the cuttings are small, otherwise they will lie on the grass and smother it.

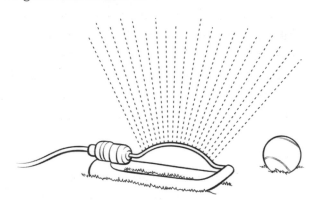

FIVE-POINT LAWN CARE PLAN

Do this in the autumn. It will help your lawn recover from summer drought and make it more drought-resistant the following year.

1 **Rake**
Yes, a thatch is a kind of roof – but it's also the name for the mat of dried-up grass clippings and other debris that can collect on the surface of the lawn, smothering the grass. Grab your lawn rake and go for it, scraping up all the unwanted material. For those in the trade, this is known as 'scarifying'. Gather the scrapings into piles and put them on the compost heap. If your lawn is large, you may need to hire a mechanical scarifier.

2 Aerate

Now grab your garden fork and push it into the soil to a depth of at least 10 cm (4 in). Repeat all over the lawn at intervals of about 10 cm (4 in). Yes, it is hard work but just think what it will do for your biceps! Aerating the lawn in this way loosens compacted soil and allows air and water to penetrate to the roots. Alternatively, use a special hollow-tined aerator that will lift out little cylinders of soil. Again, for larger lawns, hire a mechanical aerator.

3 Dress

Apply a top dressing of six parts medium-fine sand, three parts sieved soil and one part peat substitute or leaf mould, at a rate of 3 kg per square metre ($6^1/2$ lb per square yard). This levels the surface, keeps the lawn open and aerated, and aids drainage.

4 Weed

Hand-weed where possible. If using a weedkiller (check whether this is incorporated in the proprietary lawn feed), don't apply to drought-affected turf in autumn but use in spring, after feeding. Scrape up moss or treat with a moss killer, in autumn or spring.

5 Feed

Apply a proprietary autumn lawn fertilizer. This will be high in phosphorous and potassium (to encourage strong roots) and low in nitrogen (which encourages leaf growth). If it doesn't rain soon after, water your lawn.

FAIRY RINGS

Have the Little Folk paid you a visit? Is that circle of lush green grass, with toadstools on the outside and dead grass in the middle, *really* the place where fairies have come to dance in a ring? That may be what your mother told you but in fact 'fairy rings' are caused by fungi, not fairies. Your only options are either to keep your lawn fed, watered and green so the ring won't be so obvious, or dig out a band of the infested soil at least 20 cm (8 in) deep, and from 50 cm (20 in) wider on either side than the circle. Refill the gap with fresh topsoil and reseed.

ALTERNATIVE LAWNS

- If you don't want to bother with much lawn care, why not try a flowery meadow instead? Sow wild flower seeds into the grass, let it grow long and mow pathways through it.

- For a truly care-free lawn you could always go kitsch and lay artificial turf! The manufacturers say it looks convincing and it's great for roof gardens, which can't take much weight. The most famous brand, AstroTurf, was invented back in 1965 by James M. Faria and Robert T. Wright, employees of Monsanto. Originally sold as 'Chemgrass', it was first used at the Houston Astrodome stadium in 1966, after which it was renamed AstroTurf.

HEDGE YOUR BETS

Not only do they contribute colour and form to the garden, but hedges also offer shelter for other plants. In windy places, solid walls or fences can create turbulence on the sheltered side; because of their more open nature, hedges allow the movement of air through them while still acting as effective windbreaks.

WHICH HEDGE?

Whatever you decide to grow, dig the soil deeply, incorporating plenty of well-rotted organic matter. Water the hedge well in its first season, especially if the weather is dry. Here are some considerations to weigh up when deciding which hedging plant to choose.

Formal or informal?

Plants for formal clipped hedges – the kind you find in mazes – would include the traditional yew or box, while rugosa roses or bamboo will create a looser, more informal screen that won't need clipping.

Evergreen or deciduous?

Some hedging plants, like holly, stay green all year, while others turn gold in autumn but retain their leaves. It's a matter of taste and style.

Fast- or slow-growing?

A fast-growing hedging plant may seem a tempting option because you'll get results more quickly. But as it won't conveniently stop growing just when it reaches the height you want, you'll have to keep clipping. A slower-growing species might be better if you want to put in less work.

Convenience or cost?

Buying larger plants from the garden centre will give you a hedge sooner, but will cost more. Hedging sold in pots, which can be planted out at any time of year, will also cost more than 'bare root' plants, which have been grown in fields and dug up in the autumn for planting out soon after.

ALMOST INSTANT HEDGE

Place two rows of 2.5-m (8-ft) canes in the ground: the canes should be 15 cm (6 in) apart, with a distance of 60 cm (2 ft) between the rows. Cross the canes at the top to form a V-shape, and secure to another cane laid horizontally in the V. Plant two runner beans at the base of each cane. When seedlings appear, remove the weaker of the two. (Or sow a few extra seeds in a 'nursery' at the end of the rows and use the seedlings to fill any gaps in your screen.) Allow the beans to scramble up the canes, nipping off the tops when they have reached the desired height, and you'll soon have a leafy green screen, with pretty red or white flowers – and edible beans as a bonus.

WILDLIFE HEDGE

Why not grow a hedge to tempt bees, butterflies and birds to your garden? Choose different shrubs that produce food for wildlife, in the form of flowers and berries, and plant them close together in a row.

SHAPE UP!

Topiary is the art of clipping evergreen hedging plants into fantastical shapes. It has been used in both grand gardens and smaller cottage ones. Real topiary takes time, skill and a steady hand but you can cheat and produce your own. Use old hanging baskets as topiary frames. For a 'hen' or 'peacock', turn a basket upside down for the body, add wire shapes for the head and tail and train ivy over it. Or bind two baskets together with wire to make a sphere and grow ivies over it to make a green globe.

A-MAZING!

The most ambitious use of hedging is, of course, found in hedge mazes. The most famous is probably the maze at Hampton Court Palace, near London. It was laid out as part of the palace gardens for King William of Orange between 1689 and 1695. But the twentieth century has produced two monster mazes.

English monster maze

Twisting and turning for nearly 3 km (2 miles), the hedge maze on the Longleat estate in Wiltshire, England, is 2.4 m (8 ft) high, made up of more than 16,000 yew trees and covers 0.6 hectares (1$^{1}/_{2}$ acres) of countryside. It can take over an hour and a half to walk through it and even the gardeners need a couple of years to learn the route in and out. Twice a year, six gardeners spend a month trimming it by hand.

Irish monster maze

The Peace Maze at Castlewellan Forest Park, County Down, Northern Ireland covers an area of 1.1 hectares (2.7 acres) and the path between the hedges runs for 3 km (2 miles). It was constructed in 2000 using 6,000 yew trees, which were planted by people from all over Northern Ireland.

GROW YOUR OWN

If you have never grown your own vegetables before, you're in for a treat! Home-grown veg provide a taste experience that commercially grown ones rarely do, and at a fraction of the price. And what could be more wonderful than picking your own supper, grown by your own hand?

SALAD DAYS

Say goodbye to bags of soggy salad leaves that you've had to throw away only a day or two after buying them. Instead, grow your own! They'll be fresher and more nutritious, taste infinitely better and be infinitely cheaper, and they'll go on giving you leaves for much longer. You can sow the seeds any time from spring to summer or, if you cover the plants to protect them, you can even sow in autumn for a winter crop. Apart from traditional lettuces, such as butterhead, cos and iceberg, there are cut-and-come-again varieties, like bijou, with its dark-red leaves, as well as loose- and oak-leaf types, not to mention radicchio, endive and rocket.

SALAD FROM SCRATCH

1 Choose your seeds: you can buy seeds of a single type, or ready-mixed packets which will produce a variety of leaves for a mixed salad from one sowing.

2 Choose a site in sun or part-shade. Dig the soil, removing any stones, then incorporate some garden compost or well-rotted manure to provide plenty of nourishment and help

retain moisture. Rake the soil over to produce a fine tilth (fine grains of soil).

3 Draw a cane or other implement across the soil to make shallow grooves in it about 30 cm (12 in) apart, 1.5 cm (^{1}/$_2$ in) deep and no more than 60 cm (2 ft) long. Tip some seeds into your hand, take a pinch and sprinkle them thinly along the groove. Cover with soil, label and water.

4 When the seedlings are about 2 cm (1 in) tall, thin them out to 15–30 cm (6–12 in) apart to give them space to spread, depending on their variety. Make sure you keep the soil just moist, especially near harvesting. Dry soil will cause the plants to 'bolt' – produce flowers at the expense of leaves.

5 Pick leaves from cut-and-come-again varieties when the plants are about 5 cm (2 in) tall, or wait till they are 15 cm (6 in) tall and cut off the whole head, leaving a 2-cm (1-in) stump from which a new plant will sprout. Pick leaves from loose-leaf lettuces regularly to encourage continued growth. Harvest other lettuces by cutting them off at the base or pulling up the whole plant.

Top Tip

To prevent yourself being inundated with salad crops, don't sow all the seeds at once. Sow short rows every two weeks for a continuous supply.

Top Tip

Slugs are particularly partial to lettuce. However, it seems they are less fond of the varieties with red in their leaves, so these will be more trouble-free.

COSTWISE

Seeds are the cheapest option but if you want your salad leaves in a hurry, buy seedlings instead. Do bear in mind, though, that the varieties on offer will be more limited than with seeds.

IN THE FLOWER GARDEN

Have you ever noticed how pretty some vegetables are? If you haven't got space for a separate vegetable plot, why not fit some in the flower beds?

- As long as they have enough light, lettuces are great at filling in the space between other plants. With their frilly leaves, some even look like flowers. Try red or green salad bowl, lusciously red lollo rosso, or firebird, a bright-red radicchio variety.

- Sweetcorn looks like an exotic ornamental grass. Plant in blocks rather than rows, as sweetcorn is wind-pollinated which means that the pollen must be blown from one plant to another, rather than carried by bees.

- With its decorative, thick red or yellow stems, Swiss chard is much too good-looking to confine to the vegetable plot – grow it as an edible ornamental among your flowers.

- With their flower-like heads, members of the cabbage family also mix and match well with non-edible flowering plants. Try curly kale or Savoy cabbage.

CONTAINER CROPS

No garden? No worries! Grow your vegetables in containers instead – even a balcony can support a few of these, and a window-box can become a mini-vegetable plot. Choose pots that will be large enough for the eventual size of your plants – 20–47 cm (8–17 in) wide is ideal. Root vegetables will need deep pots, while top-heavy plants like tomatoes need big ones to balance their weight. And if you can't afford to buy pots, have a look at pages 42–4 for some brilliant ideas for free – or nearly free – containers. Fill them with soil-based potting compost because this retains moisture better and, if possible, mix in some water-retaining crystals, as compost in pots is more susceptible to drying out than soil in the open ground. You'll need to water more often than if you were growing crops in beds. For the plumpest, fattest fruits, feed fruiting crops with a high-potash feed once the flowers form.

Try compact plants like:

- sweet peppers, chilli peppers and aubergines (in a warm spot and supported with canes)

- courgettes

- tumbling varieties of tomatoes (good for window-boxes or hanging baskets)

- beetroot, carrots and potatoes (in deep containers)

- loose-leaf lettuces (because you pick only a few leaves at a time rather than taking the whole head, so the plants still look decorative)

Top Tip

Terracotta pots look wonderful but can absorb water. To prevent the potting compost drying out, line the pot with polythene, making sure to pierce some holes in the bottom for drainage.

BAGS OF GOODNESS

No digging, no soil preparation – what more could you ask? Growing bags are the ultimate in instant gardening, and a single bag – measuring just 35 × 95 cm (13 × 37 in) – can support three vegetable plants or a row of salad crops. When you get your bag home:

1 Pierce drainage holes in the bottom, then shake and knead the bag to loosen the compost, and shape it into a low mound.

2 If you are growing individual plants, cut out the marked squares on the top. If you are growing a row, cut a single rectangle along the length.

3 Plant or sow your vegetables (at the correct time of year, of course). Like other containers, growing bags are suitable for shallow-rooting crops such as tomatoes, cucumbers, courgettes, peppers, aubergines, broad beans, or salad vegetables such as endive, lettuce, basil and rocket. Water in well, and label.

4 Tie taller plants with canes when they are 20 cm (8 in) high, pushing the canes in next to each plant and attaching them to a frame.

5 Keep the plants well watered, feed and, when ready, harvest and enjoy!

Top Tip

*When your growing bag has done its job, recycle it.
Turn the compost out onto the soil in your garden
and use as a soil conditioner.*

*I used to visit and revisit it a dozen times a day, and stand
in deep contemplation over my vegetable progeny with a
love that nobody could share or conceive of who had never
taken part in the process of creation. It was one of the most
bewitching sights in the world to observe a hill of beans
thrusting aside the soil, or a row of early peas just peeping
forth sufficiently to trace a line of delicate green.*

**FROM MOSSES FROM AN OLD MANSE
BY NATHANIEL HAWTHORNE**

Really rich

For a really rich growing medium that plants such as tomatoes
will love, use a compost bag instead of a growing bag. Shake the
bag to break up any large clumps of compost, then cut a large
rectangle from one side of the bag to expose the compost, and
plant into this.

Before and after

- Tomatoes absorb water quickly so are best picked *before* drenching, because drenching literally 'waters down' their intense fruity flavour.

- The high water content of salad crops is what gives them their succulence and crispness, so harvest a few hours *after* drenching them. That way, they'll have had a chance to absorb the water.

BEAN THERE, DONE THAT

Racing to a giddy height of around 3 m (10 ft) in just one season, runner beans are the giants of the legume family – which includes all peas and beans – and they really have it all:

- Highly decorative, they sport a profusion of lush foliage and pretty red or white flowers that are a magnet to bees.

- They crop so prolifically you'll have to freeze some of your harvest, or give it away to grateful neighbours.

- Because of their fast, thick growth, you can use them as an almost instant 'hedge' or leafy screen while you are waiting for slower-growing hedging plants to catch up.

- Infinitely accommodating, they will grow happily in the ground or in containers.

- Even when they have done cropping, their bounty doesn't stop. Like all legumes, runner beans have nodules on their roots that store nitrogen. Along with potash and phosphorus, nitrogen is one of the key nutrients that all plants need for healthy growth. So don't dig them up at the end of the season – trim the plants back but leave the roots in the soil to enrich it.

Food and water

Runner beans have to work hard and are hungry, thirsty plants. Help them to give you their best by ensuring that they have a rich soil to grow in, and keep them well watered, especially when the flowers are forming (*see page 94*). The flowers will drop if the soil around the roots dries out – and will never form beans. If you are growing them in containers, use a soil-based compost as this is better at retaining moisture, adding in some water-retaining granules for good measure.

Frame it

Runner beans need supports to scramble up. Construct wigwams of tall bamboo canes, or make a long A-frame, with pairs of canes along the length, criss-crossing them near the top to create a V-shape and slotting another cane or canes into the V. Tie with garden string to secure. Alternatively, string pea or bean netting along the frame for the plants to climb up.

BEAN LORE

Have you ever thought how often 'beans' occurs in popular terms or sayings? Try using some of these to impress – and confuse – your family and friends:

Bean-feast: originally a feast given by an employer to his staff, probably so called because beans or a bean-goose (a migratory bird with a bean-like mark on its bill) were a favourite at such meals.
Full of beans: in spirited form.
I'll give him beans: I'll give him a thrashing.
He knows how many beans make five: he is no fool.
Every bean has its black: everyone has their faults (because every bean has a black eye).
Beans: money, property.
Without a bean: penniless.
To spill the beans: to give away a secret.

Top Tip

Why should tomatoes be the only ones to benefit from their own special fertilizer? Tomato fertilizer is high in potash which encourages fruiting, so use it to feed other fruiting vegetables too.

HOW MUCH WATER?

Leafy and salad vegetables, such as spinach and lettuce, need frequent watering to help them crop heavily and to prevent bolting (sending up early flowering shoots). The most critical period is 3–1$^1/2$ weeks before maturity. If the weather is dry during this time, water heavily once a week, applying 22 litres per square metre (5 gallons per square yard). At other times apply half this amount weekly.

Fruiting crops, such as tomatoes, peppers and beans, are especially in need of a drink when the flowers and fruits are forming. If the weather is dry during this period, water weekly, as for leafy crops. Prior to this, though, water more lightly as excess watering early on will encourage leaf growth rather than the delicious fruits you are after.

Root crops, such as carrots and radishes, should be watered at a rate of 5 litres per square metre (1 gallon per square yard) during the growing period. When the roots start to swell, give them four times this much water in dry spells.

COMPANION PLANTING

This cunning – and green – idea involves growing plants that pests like – or hate – in among your favourite carrots, cabbages, tomatoes, or whatever your prize crop happens to be. Some have a scent that deters pests, while others are so irresistible to the enemy that they will bypass your vegetables to feast on the companion plant instead. You can use the idea in the flower garden too.

French marigolds with tomato plants: the marigolds will deter aphids.

Carrots with leeks: both have strong scents that will deter each other's pests.

Nasturtiums with cabbages: who wants cabbage when you can chomp on nasturtiums instead? Caterpillars will be putty in your hands.

Garlic or chives with other plants: the pungent scent of these two members of the onion family will ward off aphids.

Dill with other plants: dill attracts aphid-eating hoverflies.

Hops with other plants: hops attracts ladybirds, which eat aphids.

TOMATO TIPS

- Remove any side shoots from tomato plants to encourage them to produce fruit – but don't throw the shoots away. Place them in compost under the parent plants for shade, and they'll root and give you new tomato plants for free!

- If you have a glut of green tomatoes at the end of the season, store them with some bananas. Bananas produce a chemical that helps other fruits to ripen.

BIGGER . . . AND BETTER?

- In September 2005, a monster marrow was exhibited at the Shepton Mallet agricultural show in Somerset, England. It weighed 62 kg (136 lb) and it took two men to carry it.

- In September 2007, Joe Jutras of Rhode Island, USA, weighed a pumpkin he had grown – it came in at 766 kg (1689 lb)!

THE HOME HERBALIST

Herbs are perhaps the oldest cultivated plants of all, prized for their medicinal and culinary properties. Growing your own herbs can be a real pleasure. You can design a whole herb bed in the style of the old kitchen gardens, or go for a pot or two by the kitchen door.

LIGHT AND SHADE

You may have given up on the idea of growing herbs because the only patch you've got is shaded for part of the day and you've been told that herbs need full sun. Not true! Many prefer light shade – even basil likes partial shade at midday.

Sun-worshippers
Drought-tolerant herbs revel in sunshine, and include lavender, thyme, sage, rosemary, French tarragon, oregano and chives.

Shady characters
Rocket, parsley, chervil and mustard are among the herbs that prefer a shadier spot. Here, the soil is less likely to dry out, keeping their roots the way they like it – nice and moist. Happy roots means happy plants that won't bolt – start to flower prematurely – and that consequently will focus their energy into producing a better leaf crop.

A KING'S GARDEN

One of the earliest-known herb gardens was created nearly 3000 years ago in Babylon, by King Mardukapal-Iddina II. It included sixty-four species, some of which we still grow today, such as coriander, dill and fennel.

TLC FOR HERBS

Herbs grown in containers and window-boxes need a little extra attention:

- Grow them in a soil-based compost. Apart from the environmental concerns regarding the use of peat, few herbs are happy growing in a peat-based medium and a soil-based compost retains moisture better – essential to stop containers drying out.

- Water in the morning rather than the evening because this will help the plants get through the day if it's hot, especially if grown in full sun.

- To keep them healthy and help them produce leaves, give the herbs a weekly feed from the beginning of spring through to the end of summer. A seaweed-based feed is good, but any proprietary feed that boosts leaf production is fine too.

GROWING OPTIONS

Try these unusual and decorative ways of growing herbs.

Strawberry planter
Grow ten different varieties in a strawberry planter – one of those large pots with planting holes around the side.

Hanging Basket
Grow herbs in a hanging basket. Lavender and thyme are a good mix. Although they are both drought-tolerant, the basket will need watering regularly, like all containers, so ease your task by mixing water-retaining crystals into the compost when planting and use slow-release fertilizer to feed them as they grow. Locate the basket in a sheltered spot where you will be able to take a reviving sniff every time you pass. At the end of the summer, plant out these perennials in the ground, to give you pleasure for seasons to come.

Pyramid

Short on space? Grow your herbs in a herb pyramid! Because it takes up little ground space, you can locate it near the kitchen door, handy for picking leaves for cooking. But take care: put your pyramid together in situ – once it is filled it will be very heavy to move.

1 Start with a large pot and half fill with John Innes No. 3 compost. Add some grit for extra drainage – herbs like a well-drained soil.

2 Place a second, smaller pot on top. It should leave a wide enough border for planting in the first pot. Top up the first pot with more compost to create the first planting 'tier'.

3 Repeat the process with a third smaller pot to fit inside the second one.

4 Plant up with your favourite herbs. Turn regularly to give all the herbs an equal amount of sun.

NO FLIES ON ME!

Basil is said to repel house flies. Grow some in a container near the kitchen door and give flies the brush-off.

HOLD YOUR NOSE

In the days before proper drainage, English cities could get . . . well, a bit smelly. So a new post was created, that of Royal Herb-strewer. It was this person's job to scatter aromatic herbs and flowers on the floors of the royal apartments to mask the city smells. When walked on, they released their scents. The first person to hold the post was Bridget Rumney, who worked from 1660–71 for King James II. Altogether she received £24 a year, plus two yards of superfine scarlet cloth for livery. The insect-repelling properties of herbs were also put to good use in stables, where they helped to repel fleas and ticks from the animals.

ROOT IT OUT

Mint is an invasive herb and will romp through any patch where it is planted. For this reason, many people plant it in pots to restrict its roots – however the roots may die off if mint is grown in this way. To prevent this happening, repot your mint every year, dividing the root ball if it has become too big, and replanting in two separate containers.

TWO FOR THE PRICE OF ONE

Many supermarkets sell potted herbs in their vegetable section. When you get your herb home, tip it out of its flimsy plastic container and transfer it to a more substantial pot. Supermarket herbs are raised quickly for a quick sale and the plants haven't had time to develop good, strong roots, so place the newcomer in a warm position and keep the compost moist until the plant is fully rooted.

KEEP GOING

For long-lasting herbs that will keep you supplied all summer, you need to know how to harvest them – get it wrong, and they'll die off before their time.

- Herbs that produce leaves along the stem, such as bay, thyme and mint, should be nipped off where the leaf meets the stem.

- Herbs that have long stems shooting up from the base, such as parsley or chives, should be cut near the base of the stems with scissors or a knife (as if you are pruning them).

- Herbs with soft leaves, such as basil or parsley, should be picked before flowers start to form. Once they reach this stage, all the plant's energy will be going into producing flowers and then seed, and the leaves will either become tough and sour, or no new ones will grow.

THE SCENTS OF SUMMER

If you want to bring the scents of summer to your food in the depths of winter, why not freeze some of the herbs you have grown?

1 Wash the leaves and carefully chop them.

2 Pour water into an ice tray until each compartment is a quarter full.

3 Top up with the chopped herb, and freeze.

4 When you want to use, just pop a cube or two into the pan. The ice will melt, releasing the flavour of fresh herbs into your dish.

GETTING FRUITY

Vegetables may seem less daunting to grow than fruit but think about it: unlike most veg, which are annuals needing to be started from scratch each year, fruit grows on perennial plants, bushes and trees and, with a little care, will keep on cropping year after year. Even a small garden will have some space for the odd plant or bush.

THE QUEEN OF BERRIES

Strawberries must be everybody's favourite berry fruit. They get their name from the straw that is traditionally used as a mulch underneath them, to hold them off the ground and reduce snail and slug damage (well, if you were a slug, wouldn't you enjoy a strawberry feast?). The taste of home-grown fruits, eaten immediately after picking, is true gastronomic heaven, so go on – find a corner in your garden or on your balcony for a few plants.

A basket full
With pretty white flowers and attractive leaves, strawberry plants are decorative enough to grow in hanging baskets. Growing them this way takes up little space and also ensures they're kept out of the way of slugs.

- Plant five to six plants in a basket in spring, and water every day during the growing season.

- From the time they flower until the fruit is ready to pick, feed the plants every ten days with a product that's high in potassium, such as a tomato feed.

- Check the plants every other day during the ripening period, and pick the fruit as soon as it's ready so it doesn't rot on the plant. The berries are ripe when they have turned red, although different varieties go different colours. It's best to harvest the fruit in dry weather, picking gently to avoid bruising it and making sure that each berry retains its calyx (its green stalk and little cap of leaves).

- The same plants should continue to produce fruit the following year, but the crop will be better if you renew the plants.

On the run

You'll notice that your strawberry plants produce long shoots with little nodules and leaves on them. These are the 'runners' from which you can get new plants absolutely free! Choose a runner with healthy green leaves and gently press into the soil or into a pot filled with multipurpose compost, pinning it in position with a U-shaped staple or piece of wire. It will form roots at the point where it is in contact with the soil. When the new plant is strongly rooted, it can be severed from the parent.

Goldilocks, Goldilocks, wilt thou be mine?
Thou shalt not wash dishes nor yet feed the swine,
But sit on a cushion and sew a fine seam,
And feed upon strawberries, sugar and cream.
TRADITIONAL NURSERY RHYME

Tug of war

To test if a strawberry plant is planted firmly enough, gently tug on one of the leaves – if the plant comes up you will need to replant it more firmly.

ACID LOVERS

Some of the most delectable berries were once the wild fruits of forest and heath. In their natural habitat, they rooted in acid soil and so are not at their happiest in garden beds, which are often too alkaline for their taste. However, by growing them in containers you can mimic their original conditions, filling the containers with acid ericaceous compost and watering them with rainwater, not tap water.

Cranberries

Rich in vitamin C and delicious in home-made sauce, cranberries are low-growing, shallow-rooting, creeping shrubs that do best in damp, acidic soil and make ideal ground cover between other acid-loving plants such as rhododendrons. If you don't have naturally acidic soil, you could go to the bother of digging a sunken bed, lining it with perforated black plastic and filling in with ericaceous compost. But really, isn't life too short? It's much easier to grow them in pots or hanging baskets. They will trail decoratively over the edge and their delicate spring flowers and colourful autumn foliage are pretty to look at.

- Just four cranberry plants in a basket will provide a family with a year's worth of berries. Ensure that you buy mature plants: most varieties won't produce a good crop of berries until they are at least two years old.

- You won't need to prune them, but do make sure to water them well (always mimic a plant's original habitat, remember?), and feed lightly every month during the growing period.

Blueberries
The classic ingredient of blueberry pie and blueberry muffins, antioxidant-rich blueberries are now on the 'wonder foods' list. Like cranberries, they need an acid growing medium, so grow them in pots of ericaceous compost (they are too big for baskets).

GROWING TREE FRUIT

Even the smallest garden can include a fruit tree. The eventual size of the tree depends on the rootstock onto which it has been grafted (joined). Plant breeders have produced dwarf varieties of many fruiting trees, but check whether the one you want is self-fertile; some trees will only produce fruit if they have a suitable pollinator nearby, whose pollen they 'share' to become fertile.

Fan it out

For the smallest of spaces, try a fan-trained tree that will grow flat against a wall or fence. In colder climates, growing a fruit tree, such as a peach, against a sunny wall will give it additional shelter and warmth because the bricks will retain heat from the day to act like a mini-radiator.

A tub's worth

Plant growers have even developed mini-bush fruit trees for growing in tubs on the patio.

LIFE IS JUST . . .

. . . a bowl of cherries. And that's exactly what you'll get if you grow your own sweet cherry tree. Or to be more exact, you'll have bowls and bowls of these scrumptious, juicy fruits, all for the price of the initial plant and a bit of manure to enrich the soil. Picked straight from the branches, they'll taste better than anything you can buy. Sweet cherries are especially easy to grow, especially if you buy a self-fertile variety which pollinates itself (if it's self-sterile, you'll need two trees to pollinate each other and produce fruit). Get advice from a reliable garden centre or fruit nursery as to the best variety for your needs. Wait till the fruits are wine-dark red and oozing juice before picking.

FRUIT LOVERS

They're fat, they're juicy, they're ripe for picking, but you may have a race on your hands to get to the fruit on your trees before others do.

A bit of bling

Who would have thought that birds can be real pests in the garden? Birds are especially fond of certain fruits such as cherries, as well as vegetables from the brassica family (cabbages, cauliflowers, Brussels sprouts and broccoli). Keep them at bay by hanging old CDs or strips of kitchen foil in the tree or above the veg. As these bits of bling move, they will glitter and sparkle and scare off your feathered fiends. It's a much easier deterrent than netting the whole tree in the traditional way.

I value my garden more for being full of blackbirds than of cherries, and very frankly give them fruit for their songs.
JOSEPH ADDISON

Beer jars

If you have an apple, pear or plum tree in your garden, you can prevent wasps burrowing into the fruit by enticing them away with an even more delicious treat. Half fill jam jars with beer mixed with sugar or some sliced fruit and hang them from the branches. Cover the jar tops with waterproof paper and tie it in place. Make a hole about 1 cm ($^1/_2$ in) wide in the top. The wasps will be attracted by the sweet concoction but, once inside, they'll struggle to get out.

STORING THE HARVEST

So you've had a bumper crop of berries and tree fruit but you can't eat it all at once, so how do you store it?

Berries

Raspberries, blackcurrants, redcurrants, blackberries and gooseberries all freeze well. Lay them out on a tray in a single layer, making sure they don't touch each other and freeze overnight. Once they are frozen, you can transfer them to an airtight plastic freezer box. The berries will stay separate. Don't bother to freeze strawberries as they will turn mushy once defrosted – just eat them as soon as you've picked them!

Tree fruits

Traditionally each fruit is wrapped in its own piece of greaseproof paper and stored in a wooden slatted box to allow air to circulate. But you don't have time for that, do you? A quicker alternative is to place them in a large polythene bag with holes pierced in the sides for aeration, spreading the fruits out in a single layer so they do not touch each other. Fruit stored in this way should be unblemished and have no signs of disease or pests. Stored in a cool, dark place it will keep for several months, but do check and discard any fruits that show signs of decay.

Top tip: How to pick apples

You can tell when apples are ready to pick by cupping one in your hand and gently twisting the stem. If it comes away from the branch easily, it is ripe.

What a whopper!

- In 2005, Chisato Iwasaki picked an apple weighing in at a record 1.8 kg (4 lb 1 oz) on his apple farm in Hirosaki City in Japan.

- But that's nothing compared to Aharon Shemoel's lemon! In 2003, Shemoel grew a lemon weighing 5.3 kg (11 lb 10 oz) on his farm in Kefar Zeitim, Israel.

TO BEE OR NOT TO BEE

A garden busy with wildlife will provide you with hours of enjoyment and moments of wonderment. By gardening organically and encouraging wildlife to your garden, you'll not only be helping to do your bit for the planet, but you'll also be making life easier for yourself. So throw away the pesticides – they can kill both friend and foe – and let Mother Nature deal with plant pests in her own way, by restoring a more healthy ratio between these creatures and their natural predators. Ladybirds, for example, will feast on the aphid population, while hedgehogs, frogs, toads and certain birds like nothing better than a dish of slugs and snails.

DO US A FAVOUR

The song of birds and the hum of bees are the soundtracks of summer. Bees are essential in a flower garden. Flowers provide bees with food in the form of nectar, while bees help to pollinate – fertilize – flowers so that they can produce seeds, berries and fruit, thus ensuring the next generation of plants. These floral temptresses attract the insects with their colour and scent and with markers that are invisible to the human eye, known as bee guides. While the bees are busy extracting nectar, some of each flower's fertilizing pollen rubs off on their legs. They then carry this pollen onto the next flower they visit. It's a two-way deal – isn't Nature clever?

DES RES

Encourage beneficial creatures to your garden by giving them somewhere to live.

Sticks and ſtones
Make a log pile by ſtacking some logs, firewood or dead branches in a quiet, damp and shady corner of your garden and allow the wood to rot down. Or pile some ſtones together and leave them undiſturbed. They may not look like much to you, but these arrangements can provide five-ſtar winter accommodation for hedgehogs, young frogs and newts, toads, ground beetles, and centipedes, which eat slugs and snails and their eggs. They also provide a welcome refuge for the globally threatened ſtag beetle.

Boxing clever
Bumblebees are easier to house than honeybees, which will need a hive. Invite them to live with you by buying a bumblebee box. This is about the size of a small bird box but has two compartments – one filled with wood shavings in which the queen breeds, and a second one for the other bees. Site it in a warm, sheltered, south-facing spot, out of direct sunlight, and close to any area where the bees might forage for food. Bumblebees also neſt in tussocks of grass or moss, so you could also leave some rough grass at the edge of your garden.

All holed up

Red mason bees are excellent fruit-tree pollinators. In the wild they often nest in holes in wood or in thick plant stems, but you can encourage them to your garden with a purpose-made box, or make your own from hollow bamboo. Fix the box to a tree or post as these bees like to nest higher up than bumblebees. It can be placed in direct sunlight but you should angle the entrance slightly downwards so that rain cannot get in.

He said the pleasantest manner of spending a hot July day was lying from morning till evening on a bank of heath in the middle of the moors, with the bees humming dreamily about among the bloom, and the larks singing high up overhead, and the blue sky and bright sun shining steadily and cloudlessly.
FROM *WUTHERING HEIGHTS* BY EMILY BRONTË

WHAT'S ON THE MENU?

It's not much good having a wonderful place to live if you can't put food on the table. Give wildlife further encouragement to come to your garden – and help to preserve threatened species – by growing their favourite foods.

- Simple, single flowers, or inflorescences (flat-headed flower heads made up of clusters of tiny florets), are more popular than complex, multi-petalled ones because the nectar is easier to access. Try yarrow (*Achillea*), mallow (*Althaea*), poppies (*Papaver*) and the 'butterfly bush' (*Buddleia davidii*).

- Flowers with deep cups, such as foxgloves, honeysuckle (*Lonicera* species) and aquilegia, are favoured by bumblebees, with their long tongues. Honeysuckle also attracts moths with its nocturnal scent, and birds eat the seeds.

- Giant sunflowers, with their chocolate-brown hearts as large as plates, are a magnet to bees in summer. In autumn, the dried seed heads, left on the tall stems, will become the neighbourhood diner for local birds.

- Proprietary bird food, laid out on bird tables (out of reach of cats!) or in feeders, is a welcome source of nourishment for birds in the lean winter months. Don't forget to top the food up as the birds may become reliant on it.

- Stinging nettles provide food for caterpillars as well as some moths, and the caterpillars in turn provide food for birds such as tits. Birds may also eat nettle seeds. For butterflies, you need a good-sized nettle patch in a sunny, sheltered position. Keep picking the nettle leaves (they make good soup) to encourage the fresh, young growth that caterpillars like.

WATCH THE BIRDY!

Along with buds on the trees, birdsong is one of the earliest indicators of the coming of spring and lifts the spirits. Help to give your feathered friends board and lodging, and they'll love coming to your garden.

HOME-MADE BIRD BOX

Although you can buy them, it can be fun making your own bird box. Do this preferably in the autumn.

You will need:

*Exterior-grade plywood or a plank,
1290 mm long, 150 mm wide
and 15 mm thick
Galvanized nails
Wood sealant
Rubber or leather strip for the hinge
Glue for attaching the hinge
Dried moss (available from garden centres)*

1 Mark out on the wood the various cuts you will need to make for the different parts. You will need a 120 mm-long piece for the floor, two sloping sides, 200 mm long on one edge and 250 mm on the other, a roof 220 mm long, a back 300 mm long

150 mm

120 mm	FLOOR
200 mm	SIDE
250 mm	SIDE
220 mm	ROOF
300 mm	BACK
200 mm	FRONT

250 mm
200 mm

and a front 200 mm long. This should use up the length of wood exactly, with no wastage.

2 Saw the wood into the pieces you have marked out. Seal the pieces inside and out to preserve the wood.

3 Drill a small hole in the floor so that waste or rainwater can drain away. Drill an entrance hole high up in the front. It should be 25 mm wide for blue and coal tits, 28 mm for great tits, and 32 mm for house sparrows. For wagtails, robins and flycatchers, which need a wide, square entrance, cut the front in half and discard the unwanted half.

4 Nail the pieces together, placing the floor a few millimetres up from the base of the back. Glue the hinge in place to fix the top flap to the back of the box. Line the bottom of the box with dried moss.

5 Drill a hole in the back and hang up the box in a shaded, sheltered position with an unobstructed flightpath, 2–3 m above the ground. Keep it away from the feeding table and competition from other birds. Now all you have to do is wait for the feathered family to arrive!

WINTER FEAST

Suet balls provide birds with the extra energy-giving fat they need during the colder months. It's easy to make your own and you can vary the recipe – the kids will enjoy making them too.

Serve these treats in winter only, as birds don't need the extra fat in summer, and higher temperatures may cause the suet to melt, go rancid, drip and damage feathers. Hang your suet treat in the shade and replace it if it gets wet.

You will need:

225 g (8 oz) beef or vegetable suet, slightly chilled
175 g (6 oz) crunchy peanut butter
75 g (3 oz) rolled oats
150 g (5 oz) cornmeal
175 g (6 oz) mixed wild birdseed

1. Roughly chop the suet, place in a saucepan and stir over a low heat, to melt.
2. Add the peanut butter and stir thoroughly to combine, then stir in the remaining ingredients.
3. Allow to cool, then pour into a mould or moulds and transfer to the refrigerator to set. You can use muffin tins lined with cupcake papers – just remove the papers when ready to 'serve', and place in a large feeder, or allow the mixture to set in a clean margarine tub and suspend the tub from a branch with a loop of string. Alternatively, dip a pine cone in the suet mixture and hang from the tree. Leftover mixture can be stored in the freezer for later use.

Variations

Vary your recipe by substituting some of the oats, cornmeal and seeds with the following:

- unsalted, finely chopped nuts

- currants or chopped raisins

BIRD DOS AND DON'TS

Don't use mesh fruit and vegetable bags as holders for bird food – the birds can get their feet caught in the mesh.

Don't put peanuts out loose on the bird table – they are too big and the birds might choke. Serve them in a special wire-mesh feeder so that the birds have to peck at them.

Don't put out breadcrumbs for the birds – they will just fill up on them, rather than eating more nutritious foods.

Do offer them other scraps such as uncooked porridge oats, breakfast cereal, grated cheese, leftover jacket potatoes, cooked rice, cake and biscuit crumbs, and pastry pieces. Over-ripe strawberries or fruit windfalls will be popular too.

Don't leave too much food out – birds are discriminating and rotting food can attract rats.

Do keep bird feeders clean and germ-free – wash them out regularly, removing any encrusted food.

DRINK UP!

Water is important for wildlife. If you can't manage a pond, even a simple, shallow bowl will allow birds and animals to drink, and dragonflies to breed. If you have cats, make sure it's out of jumping, climbing or lurking range.

POND LIFE

Water has been a key element in garden design for centuries. Reflections in the still surface or the sound of a gently trickling fountain add an extra dimension to an outside space, so it's no surprise that ponds and water features have again become popular in recent years. You may not own a huge garden, but even on a small balcony there's no reason why you can't be the proud owner of a water feature.

FORMAL OR INFORMAL?

Any pond or water feature needs to be in keeping with the size and style of your plot. When deciding, look at where you are going to locate the feature – on the terrace or balcony, or in a more natural setting, perhaps as part of a wildlife garden?

Round, square or rectangular shapes are the best choice for small urban gardens, patios or balconies. Unashamedly man-made, they become architectural features in their own right, lending an extra design element to the setting. Sink them level with the ground or paving, or choose free-standing ones, perhaps adding a wide ledge around the edges to provide extra seating. Paving slabs, bricks or old railway sleepers are all suitably formal edging materials. For smaller spaces, container ponds are an excellent choice.

Irregular shapes that mimic natural ponds look best in larger gardens and wilder settings, away from the artificiality of paved patios or decking. To enhance the illusion that they formed by themselves – without any help from you – they need to be sunk into the ground. Disguise the edges with stones, coarse gravel and clever planting.

CONTAINER OR LINER?

Whether you choose a preformed container or liner for your pond depends on various factors. Before you choose, try this little question-and-answer session:

What are my best choices for a formal or urban pond?
Go for a large concrete plant pot or large, simple terracotta or glazed pot that will give you the geometric shape you need. Seal any porous inner surfaces with resin or clear silicon (sold at builders' merchants and DIY stores). You'll also need to stop up any drainage holes: use a rubber bung (available in wine-making shops) and seal with silicon. For geometric sunken ponds, dig the appropriately shaped hole, line with a liner and edge with paving slabs or bricks. Geometric pond kits are available too, for home assembly – check out your garden centre.

What are my best choices for a natural-looking pond?
Preformed fibreglass pond shells come in irregular, natural shapes in various sizes. However, you'll be limited to what's available in the garden centre. If you want a pond the size of a lake and as deep as the ocean, dig a hole and line it with a suitable liner. Alternatively, for a rustic effect with minimum effort, try a barrel pond made from an old whisky half-barrel (available from garden centres). These come in sizes up to 1 m (3 ft) across, but 45 cm (1¹/2 ft) is more manageable.

How much hard graft am I prepared to put in?
The quickest and easiest option is a raised, free-standing pond, using an existing container. Although they may seem an easy option, preformed fibreglass shells can be the most time-consuming to install because you have to ensure that the hole you dig follows the shape of the shell and supports it perfectly – if not, the shell may crack.

How long do I want my pond to last?
As in all areas of life, you get what you pay for. PVC liners and non-rigid fibreglass shells are cheaper than rigid shells and specially treated long-life PVC and butyl rubber liners – but they have a lifespan of only five to ten years. The more expensive options can give you twenty-five years plus. Ask yourself: do you really want to have to start all over again in about five years?

BARREL OF LEAKS

To prevent leaks, fill your half-barrel with water and leave it to soak so that the wood swells and plugs up any gaps. This will also help to draw out any toxin residues left over from what the barrel previously held. Ideally, choose one at the garden centre that's full of rainwater as this will already have done much of the work for you! If you want to be absolutely sure that it won't leak, seal the seams with silicon first and paint the inside with black bitumastic paint. Leave to dry, then fill with water. Don't try to line a barrel pond – the liner will form deep folds, you won't be able to hide the edge, and it will look horrible.

HOW MUCH LINER?

Calculate the length and width you want your pond to be, then add twice the maximum depth of the pond to both figures.

ON THE LEVEL

Because water finds its own level, it is essential that the edges of your pond are level too or you will have ugly and uneven gaps between the top of the water and the top of the pond. Use a spirit level to ensure you have got it right.

CLEAN WATER

You want the water in your pond to be like a clear mirror, reflecting the sky – not a thick green 'pea soup'. The pea-soup effect is due to the presence of algae, such as duckweed – deceptively pretty little floating plants, which quickly cover the surface, smothering other plants – and blanketweed – dense, hair-like green strands growing underwater. As well as looking unsightly, they are not good news because they can lead to de-oxygenation of the water, which is detrimental to aquatic life.

What causes the 'pea soup' effect?

- Too much sunlight

- Excess nutrients getting into the pond from fertilizers or soil

- Frequent topping up with tap water

- Overfeeding fish and/or overstocking with fish

How can you cure it?

✓ Ensure that your pond is at least 75 cm (2^1/$_2$ ft) deep, as shallow pools warm up quickly in the sun, which speeds algal growth.

✓ Use black pond liners to minimize the reflection of heat into the water.

✓ Add oxygenating and other aquatic plants. Not only will they take up excess nutrients from the water but they will shade it too. Aim to have at least one third of the pool's surface covered. However, the plants will take a while to get established (a new pond takes about three seasons to settle).

✓ Add a filter that will remove nutrients and algae while you are waiting for your pond plants to establish.

✓ Add a fountain. Duckweed hates moving water.

✓ Grow watercress in your waterfall, if you have one. It will act as a natural filter as the water runs through it, starving the algae out.

✓ Pull out blanketweed and sieve out the duckweed.

✓ Use only special aquatic compost for your pond plants – ordinary soil is too rich – and top it with shingle to keep it in place and prevent it spreading.

✓ Keep the pond clean. Cover it with a net in autumn to prevent nutrient-rich leaves falling into it, and remove leaves at other times. Clean out the sludge at the bottom every few years.

✓ Add a bag or two of barleystraw (available from garden centres and aquatic specialists). As the straw decomposes, it releases chemicals that inhibit algal growth. Remove the straw when it goes black – it's job is done.

✗ Avoid topping up frequently with tap water, if possible, as this is rich in nutrients.

✗ Take care when applying fertilizer to your garden that it does not run off into your pond.

✗ Avoid overfeeding your fish or including too many, as both produce nutrient-rich waste.

Hazard warning!

Water and electricity can be dangerous together, so always plug pumps or ready-made water features into a circuit breaker that will cut the power instantly if there's a problem.

SAFETY FIRST

If you have young children, cover your pond with a metal grid and secure firmly in place. The pond plants will grow through the mesh, softening the look. Or choose a water feature that hardly contains any water, such as a pebble pool with a small fountain.

POND VISITORS

- Frogs will discover your pond by themselves and take up residence there. It's a myth that they only return to the pond where they grew up to breed. Their spawn looks like blobs of clear jelly, floating on the water.

- Toads will just visit your pond to breed, producing long thin strands of spawn which wind around water plants.

- To allow frogs and toads easy access to your pond, give it sloping sides.

- If your pond is on the large side, ensure that there are little islands of dry ground in the middle – say, stepping stones or rocks – so that any wildlife that falls in accidentally has something solid to scramble onto.

A FISHY TAIL

If you want fish in your pond . . .

- It needs to be at least 60 cm (2 ft) deep over one-third of its area. This deeper water will stay cool in hot weather but will be too deep to freeze in winter.

- Add oxygenating plants to put oxygen into the water. For smaller ponds, starwort or water violet are a good choice.

- To calculate the number of fish your pond can support: allow a 2.5 cm (1 in) length of fish, including the tail, for every 0.9 m (1 sq ft) of pond surface.

- After creating your pond, wait two to three weeks before introducing fish to allow the oxygenators to take root and the water to mature. Float the bag of fish on the surface for 20–30 minutes, open the bag to allow a little pond water in, wait 5 minutes, then tip the fish into the pond.

- Don't feed fish for their first few days in the pond – they'll be too nervous.

- If you want friendly fish, feed them at the same time in the same place every day and you'll soon find them waiting for you.

HOW MANY PLANTS?

Three plants per square metre (yard) of surface water is a good measure. Aim to cover half to two-thirds of the surface with floating plants, and half the base with oxygenators. Specialist nurseries or online suppliers have a tempting range to choose from, and can give informed advice.

BEGINNERS' ERRORS

Here are some of the most common mistakes novice pond-owners make:

1. Underestimating the size of the pond you need.

2. Overstocking the pond with fish. Fish do multiply – especially if your kids are feeding them ten times a day!

3. Not doing your research on pond design, construction and location. If you want water-lilies, the pond needs to be in the sun. On the other hand, too much sun (and topping up the pond with nutrient-rich tap water) can cause 'green water' due to presence of microscopic plants called algae.

4. Placing the pump and filters in an inaccessible place – you need to be able to reach these to clean them.

5. Planting a landscape that does not complement the pond, or siting it near trees or plants that will drop their leaves into the water, which will then rot and clog the filter on the pond pump.

6. Unknowingly adding invasive aquatic plants, such as water hyacinth. These luscious plants float on the water by means of cunning, air-filled sacs. Native to South America, some species can double their population in two weeks and have been known to block shipping lanes.

WATER MONSTERS

- In 2007, a toad with a body the size of a football and weighing nearly 0.9 kg (2 lb) was discovered in Darwin, Australia.

- In 1993, 83-year-old widow Ada Shaw, from Folkestone, Kent, in the south of England, bought a goldfish that was then a tiddly 2.5 cm (1 in) long. By 2008, fifteen years later, 'Goldie' had grown to 38 cm (1 ft 3 in) long, 12 cm (5 in) high, and more than 0.9 kg (2 lb) in weight. Goldie was only pipped to the post as the world's largest-known goldfish by another in the Netherlands measuring 48 cm (1 ft 7 in).

PESKY PETS

We love 'em, we hate 'em. They're our four-legged 'companion animals' and they bring us enormous pleasure. But in the garden, cats and dogs can wreak havoc.

GOING TO THE DOGS

Circular patches of dead brown grass, with bright-green grass growing around the edge, may be due to one of two things:

- the application of too much fertilizer, especially in dry weather, which has caused scorching
- the urine of a bitch (the correct term, perhaps in more ways than one); the urine also scorches the grass but eventually breaks down to nitrogen which feeds and 'greens' the area around the scorched patch

If your dog is the cause of the problem, you need to act quickly. Water the affected area copiously as soon as you can, and reseed later. The urine of male dogs does not cause the same problem.

TURF WARS

If your dog uses the lawn as an exercise area, the turf can become worn and compacted. Letting your pet out there in wet weather makes the problem even worse. If your lawn is going to survive, you will need to:

1 Use coarser, harder-wearing grass that can withstand the pounding.

2 Take your dog out for walks rather than just letting it loose in the garden, you lazy person.

3 Follow a more intense than usual lawn-maintenance programme.

TOILET TERRORISTS

You know that seedbed you've just spent hours digging and smoothing and sowing? To you, it's your new lawn or flower patch. To a cat, it's toilet heaven. 'What, you made the earth all lovely and soft just for me? Just so I could go to the toilet without having to hurt my delicate paws digging?' That's how a cat sees it: newly worked soil is like a magnet to moggies and find it they will. To deter them, you could opt for one of the many products available from garden centres. Or you could try one of the following DIY remedies invented by determined gardeners to keep those furry toilet terrorists away . . . while barely spending a penny!

- Hang a large wind chime next to the cats' favourite toilet spot – the bigger and noisier the better.

- A-tishoo! Sprinkle the area with chilli powder or with pepper dust, available from garden centres. You'll need to reapply after rain.

- Sprinkle citrus peel, oil of citronella or eucalyptus oil around the protected area.

- Strew crumbled mothballs around the site.

- Soak some old teabags in strong disinfectant and place around the seedbed.

- Soak the blighters. Spray them with a hose or a water pistol whenever you see them settling down to do the deed. But you'll have to catch them in the act for this to work. If you're a bit handy, you could do what some desperate gardeners have done – build your own automatic water-spray deterrent triggered by a sensor.

- If neighbouring cats are a problem, get your own cat or dog to defend your territory against these interlopers. If you don't want the real flesh-and-blood thing, you can buy cat-shaped scarers with reflective glass eyes that cats will mistake – for a time – for the genuine article, and stay away.

- Gather together all your unwanted CDs and stand them upright in the soil. The cats will see their own reflections in them and will beat a hasty retreat.

- Half fill a couple of large plastic lemonade bottles with water to prevent them blowing away, and leave them lying in the garden. For some obscure reason known only to moggies, it seems to work.

- Cover seed trays with a lid or clingfilm, or place them well out of the cat's way. Moggies are almost clairvoyant when it comes to locating the clean laundry basket so, with the same infallible instinct, they will know – for sure – that you mean the seed tray to be their new personal toilet.

- Give them their own toilet. Encourage them to 'go' in one part of the garden by turning over the soil there, and spraying around it with a feline pheromone from the vet's or a pet shop.

- Lay some prickly or thorny twigs in a grid over the area.

- As the seedlings come up, you can rearrange the twigs to allow them to grow through.

- Bury some bottles of ammonia up to their necks next to the protected area. The ammonia smells like strong urine (nice!) and will keep the moggies at bay.

- Want the ultimate top-cat territory-marker? Get yourself to the nearest zoo or safari park and buy yourself some lion or tiger dung. Zoos sell this in frozen form and suggest that you defrost and dilute a lump and apply to the garden. No feline toilet terrorist will mess with you now. The only thing you have to ask yourself is: where will you keep the rest of the frozen droppings? In the freezer with the burgers and oven chips?

HEALTH ALERT!

Dog and cat faeces can be a serious health hazard, especially to young children. Dogs infected with a worm known as *Toxocara canis* and cats infected with *Toxocara cati* excrete the eggs of the worm in their faeces. People who come into contact with these can then develop toxocariasis, an infection that, in extreme cases, can lead to blindness or even death. Cats normally bury their faeces and will leave them exposed only to show dominance or if they feel the need to assert their presence. Dogs do not bury their excrement and if you allow it to accumulate in your garden you may even be breaking the law. In Britain, for example, this would be an offence under the Environmental Protection Act 1990. Infected faeces can remain a health risk for many months.

Do take this seriously! To prevent infection:

- wear gloves for gardening and wash your hands well afterwards

- wash your hands after handling pets

- wearing rubber gloves, collect any exposed dog and cat faeces, place in a double-sealed bag and dispose of with the domestic rubbish (do *not* compost)

- teach children to wash their hands after playing outside, or with pets

- teach children not to eat soil or dirt, and to wash their hands before meals

- wash any vegetables or fruit that have come in contact with the soil

---

I once had a sparrow alight upon my shoulder for a moment, while I was hoeing in a village garden, and I felt that I was more distinguished by that circumstance than I should have been by any epaulet I could have worn.

HENRY DAVID THOREAU

PERFECT PLANNING

Don't be too daunted by the idea of planning a garden. If your plan doesn't work, you can often change things later.

AN ESTABLISHED GARDEN

If you have just moved into your home and it has an established garden, don't rush to change it. Try to be patient and live with it for a year and see what comes up. To cheer yourself up in the meantime, you can always add a few bedding plants or container plants for an instant splash of colour. Familiarize yourself with your garden:

- View it from different angles.

- Look at it from an upstairs window; this can highlight problem spots that might not be visible at ground level.

- Take photographs of it from different angles at different times of the year – it's surprising what you can spot in a two-dimensional picture that you don't in three-dimensional reality.

STARTING FROM SCRATCH

If you are starting more or less from scratch, you have the scope to include whatever you like. Familiarize yourself with the plot as above, then measure it out and start planning what you'd like to include. The following tips and tricks are worth considering:

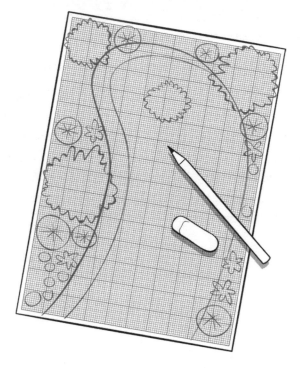

- What's your style? Cool contemporary or cottage garden? Formal or informal? Neat or natural? Your taste in home decor and clothes is a good clue to your taste in gardens. Normally, it's best that the style of your garden echoes the style of your house so that one blends seamlessly into the other.

- Whose gardens do you like? Start an ideas board of pictures culled from magazines and newspapers. Not only will this indicate your personal taste in garden design, but it's also a rich source of ideas to plunder. Visiting other gardens that are open to the public can inspire you too – and don't be afraid to ask the owner about the planting. Gardeners love talking about their gardens.

- Do you want to include a place to sit in the sun at the end of the day, or a patio for the evening?

- Where does the sun fall at different times of day?

- Where are the main areas of shade? Where is the soil dry and well drained; where is it wetter and heavier? This will influence what you can plant there. Plants that originate in hot, sunny habitats will thrive in your garden's hotspots, while those with woodland origins will be happier in cool shade. Put simply, plants do best in places that most closely mimic their original habitats.

- Do you need to screen out your surroundings?

- Do you need to make space for children to play?

- Do you want to include a herb garden or vegetable plot?

All gardening is landscape painting.
ALEXANDER POPE

AS YOU LIKE IT

The garden of painter and film-maker Derek Jarman (1942–94) is proof that your little piece of paradise can be as idiosyncratic as you like. Work on it began in 1985, after Jarman had purchased Prospect Cottage, a fisherman's cottage at Dungeness, Kent, in southern England. In this most unlikely setting – a windswept, inhospitable piece of land on a shingle beach facing a nuclear power station – Jarman used all his creative genius to create a world-famous and unique garden. Where some might have fought against the surroundings, Jarman embraced them. Rather than growing hedges to provide a sheltering screen behind which he could raise tender plants, he left his plot open to the elements and used low-growing maritime plants that could withstand the sea winds. Instead of conventional statuary, he relied on his artist's eye to adorn his garden with found objects – old fishing tackle, shells, broken garden tools, driftwood perched on-end like standing stones, and pieces of twisted metal from old sea defences. Instead of a lush lawn, there is shingle, flint and shells – all of which goes to show that anything goes, as long as you like it!

VITAL STATISTICS

Small, medium, tall
Think of your plant arrangements like a wedding photograph – with taller relatives at the back, those of medium height in the middle and little kids in the front.

Long and skinny
Break up the length of a long, narrow plot by dividing it widthways into 'garden rooms'. Use planting, hedging and trellis stretching up to halfway across – think of them as the wings on a theatrical stage.

Making it bigger

Increase the perceived size of your garden by using a classic trick: 'borrowed landscape'. Blur the boundaries with hedges and climbers so that the viewer does not know where your garden ends and neighbouring ones begin. If you are really lucky and your garden is surrounded by countryside, you can make it seem as if you have a grand estate that goes on for ever!

Top tip

If you want to screen an unsightly object, it's natural to plant a tree or erect a fence close to the offending item. However, it's much more effective to place the screen close to your main vantage point – being nearer, it will block out a wider area of view.

ALL SPACED OUT

When you buy potted perennials for planting out in your garden, don't make the mistake of planting them too close to each other. They may look small now but they won't stay small. Check their spread on the plant label, and plant accordingly. Fill the spaces inbetween with annuals.

GARDENER'S NOTEBOOK

Keep a gardening notebook throughout the year, and note down what hasn't worked – because of size, location or cultivation – and what has worked. Remember there are no mistakes, only lessons, so use the 'lessons' of last year as the basis of new experiments this year.

GLORIOUS CURVES

When creating curved beds or a lawn, it can be difficult to get a lovely, natural flowing shape if you are working along the edge only bit by bit. This is where the humble garden hose can come to your aid. Lay the hose out on the ground and arrange it into the sweeping curves that you want, then use it as your guide.

AGES OLD

New terracotta pots can look a bit brash, but you can give them more character by encouraging moss and lichens to grow on them, thus 'ageing' them artificially.

1 Soak the pot in water.

2 Paint the outside with natural yogurt.

3 Leave your pot in a damp, shady place and let Nature do the rest.

THE WONDERS OF PAINT

Stencilling a pot
Thoroughly clean the surface of your chosen unglazed terracotta pot, then paint a stencil onto it, using emulsion paint or outdoor acrylic 'patio' paint, available from DIY stores. When the paint's dry, give the pot a coat of yacht varnish to lengthen the life of the paint.

The sky's the limit
If you have a small garden enclosed by dark walls, paint the walls sky blue and you will open up the space and get that sunlit effect.

COLOUR COORDINATION

You wouldn't jumble different colours together in one room in your house, so why treat your garden any differently? Think colour coordination!

- If you have a mixed collection of wooden garden furniture, paint it all the same colour for a smart, coordinated effect.

- Give your garden a more 'designed' look by painting your plant pots the same or similar colours, or go for deliberately bold contrasts.

- Stick to a simple palette. Go for 'families' of colours, say blues and greens, or reds and oranges. If you want to paint a wall, coordinate it with the colours of your garden furniture and pots.

CARING FOR GARDEN FURNITURE

- To lengthen the life of a garden seat, turn it upside down in winter.

- Cover wooden benches with a fitted, purpose-built cover, or tarpaulin.

- Treat wooden garden furniture with teak oil, to help preserve it. Treat decking with oil, too.

ART FOR (ALMOST) FREE

You don't need to spend a fortune on garden statuary, which can often be rather boring and predictable. It's much more fun, and looks more original, to use 'found objects' to ornament your perfect plot. Junk shops and builders' skips provide rich picking grounds. Train your eye to see the potential in unexpected objects and be as creative as your imagination will allow. If your piece of garden art looks too tatty, a coat of spray paint can work wonders in evening out dents and blemishes.

Tile monster
Use broken roofing tiles or large pieces of broken terracotta pot, pushed into an area of gravel, to form the crest of a garden dragon. Get some ideas for the shape from books, then sprinkle some sand in situ to act as your guide as you push the 'crest' into place.

Bottle sculpture

Here's what to do with all those wine bottles left over from parties. Wash them, up-end them and push them into the soil in a tight group arrangement. It's a good idea to try out the arrangement on a pathway first, and adjust it accordingly.

GARDEN LIGHTING

Adding lighting can transform a garden to a magical space in the evening. Nowadays, you don't even need to worry about employing a professional electrician to install the lighting for you. There are all sorts of options that don't involve wiring:

- *Solar lights* come in all shapes and sizes. They don't need cables and they are completely movable! Just push them into the ground, in a place where they'll get enough sun to charge them.

- *Garden flares* are another option for one-off use. But don't leave them unattended.

- *Tea lights* can be placed in a variety of containers – from purpose-made lamps to old jam jars – and suspended from branches, or hooks on a wall or fence, for a really romantic look.

- *Scented garden candles*, such as those perfumed with citronella, not only give light but may also deter the biting insects that are abroad on summer evenings.

Starlit garden

Light pollution and cloudy skies can obscure the stars, so why not introduce your own? You'll need some of those glow-in-the-dark stars children like in their bedrooms, ideally the more substantial ones. Some come with an adhesive already attached, but you may need to use extra glue to get them to adhere firmly to a wall, somewhere near the patio where you can easily see them. They'll charge themselves up with sunlight during the day but if they need a boost at night, just shine a torch onto them. Magic!

SMALL BUT PERFECTLY FORMED

Your garden may be small, or you may have no more than a balcony, roof terrace or window sill – but there is no reason why you still can't enjoy the benefits of gardening. Here's how to make the most of your small space.

TROMPE L'ŒIL

This fancy French phrase simply means 'trick the eye' and you can trick the eye to great effect in a small garden to make it seem bigger than it really is.

Mirror, mirror
Borrow a clever interior designer's trick and use a mirror to increase the perception of space. Fix a large mirror to a fence or wall at the end of your plot and surround it with an arch of greenery and flowers to disguise the edges. The mirror will reflect the garden, tricking the eye into believing that what it sees is more garden through the archway.

More than meets the eye
Take a tip from garden design in Japan, where space is often at a premium. Instead of opening out their plots so that everything can be viewed in a single sweep, Japanese gardeners often screen

off parts of the garden, creating the visual illusion that there is a whole lot more 'around the corner' than meets the eye.

Hot and cold

As any artist or interior designer will tell you, hot colours appear to advance towards the eye, while cooler colours recede. To create a greater sense of depth in a small garden, have plants with orange, red and other 'hot' flowers close to, and blues, mauves and whites further down the garden.

Going, going, gone

To make a short garden seem longer, use perspective to trick the eye. Perspective is the visual illusion whereby objects seem smaller the further away they are. Here's how:

- Make paths taper inwards as they reach the back of the garden.

- Place a large urn or statue close to the house and a smaller one at the end.

- Arrange plants so they decrease in size the further down the garden they are.

- Make a fence or hedge at the end of the garden lower than those at the sides.

INNER CITY, OUTER SPACE

If you yearn for a peaceful green haven in the hustle and bustle of city life but have no garden, take a tip from King Nebuchadnezzar, who produced the ultimate 'gardens in the air' – the Hanging

Gardens of Babylon – and design your own hanging garden on a balcony or flat roof. But there are some important considerations before you get going . . .

Don't get weighed down
Wet soil can weigh as much as 36 kg (80 lb) per 0.1sq m (1 sq ft), so weight is an important issue if you are planning a roof garden in particular.

✓ Check with an architect or structural engineer to find out how much weight the roof can take. If you are planning to have more than a few pots and the odd chair and table out there, leave it to the professionals to design it for you.

✓ Check with a builder to find out whether the roof is sufficiently waterproof.

✓ Check with your local authority whether you need planning permission to create a roof garden, or whether there are any building regulations you need to meet – these exist to protect you and the structure of your home.

Shelter from the storm
Balconies and rooftops are more exposed than ground-level sites, so add trellis or other lightweight screening to shelter yourself and your plants from strong sunshine and wind. Ensure that these are well supported and firmly attached.

Lighten up
Reduce the load your roof or balcony has to carry:

• Use plastic or fibreglass plant pots rather than heavier terracotta. Choose from the traditional terracotta look, or go for fake stone or lead planters. One or two larger containers will make more of a statement than a lot of smaller ones.

- Fill the pots with soilless compost or special lightweight roof-garden compost.

- Locate the pots near load-bearing walls, or over a load-bearing joist.

Managing the watering

To guard against containers drying out more quickly because of the extra exposure on rooftops and balconies:

- Use plastic or fibreglass containers as these retain more moisture than unglazed terracotta, which soaks it up.

- See if you can run a gutter pipe along the overhang of your balcony, leading to a small rain barrel, to give you water on tap. Balconies often have an overhang designed to protect you from rain – but that means rain won't be getting to your plants either.

What plant?

Direct sunlight and higher winds can make your garden in the clouds a tough place for plants, so choose hardy ones. Those that are drought-tolerant will do especially well.

THE DECKCHAIR GARDENER

Keen gardeners like nothing more than getting out there and getting stuck in – weeding, potting, transplanting, pruning, dividing and doing all those other tasks that keen gardeners do to achieve horticultural perfection. But be honest: do you really want to slave away over a hot flower bed, or would you rather sit in your deckchair, admiring the view? How can you savour the pleasures of the garden while avoiding the pain? Read on.

TIME IS MONEY

When it comes to the garden, as in so many other areas of life, time is money! If cost is your prime concern, you can save a great deal by raising the plants yourself from seed, but that will take time and effort. If you don't want to spare the time, you can pop down to your local swanky garden centre and spend a fortune on plants that have already been conveniently potted up for you. All you'll need to do when you get them home is dig a hole in the ground, turn them out of their pots, pop them into the ground and – hey presto! – instant garden. Time or money? The choice is yours.

THE AYES HAVE IT

One of the major ways you can limit the amount of gardening you have to do is in your choice of plants.

Say yes to . . .
Plants that more or less take care of themselves:

- Conifers, which can give structure to a garden and which change colour in the winter, depending on species

- Shrubs, including evergreens, which give structure, texture with differing leaf shapes, and flowers (some are even scented)

- Herbaceous perennials, provided they don't need staking or tying up, or lots of deadheading

- Grasses, the ultimate low-maintenance perennials, which add visual interest and movement to the garden, need no staking, tying up or deadheading, and require cutting down only once a year

- Ferns, needing very little care

- Flowering bulbs that don't need lifting and that come up year after year (go for ones that don't have floppy foliage that looks messy once flowering is over)

Say maybe to . . .
Plants that require a little work:

- Any woody perennials, such as roses or buddleias, that you have to prune once a year

- Resilient hardy annuals that you can grow from seed, scattered directly on the ground

- Bedding plants or plants in pots that you just turn out and pop into a hole in the soil

- Lawns, which will need cutting once a week in the growing season

- Vegetables, which do require a bit of attention

- Hedges, which need trimming regularly

- Plants in pots, which need watering more often than plants in the soil

Say no to . . .
Plants that need fussing and fretting over:

- Tender perennials which, in colder climates, need to be cut back and covered over in winter, or lifted and stored, to protect them from frost

- Any bulbs, corms or tubers that need lifting in winter

- Flowering plants that have to be grown under glass and transplanted when the weather is warmer

- Bare-root roses (you'll need to soak the roots and dig a specially shaped hole with a mound in the middle on which to rest the roots)

- Plants that are especially susceptible to particular diseases, such as roses that are prone to black spot and will need regular spraying to keep the disease in check, or will end up bald – a sad, leafless, mass of stems

- Herbaceous perennials that need staking or tying up, deadheading and cutting down at the end of the growing season

CATALOGUE SPEAK

What the gardening catalogues say . . . and what they mean:

- 'Carefree' refers more to the plant's attitude than to the amount of work it will demand from you.

- 'Vigorous' is code for 'has a Napoleonic compulsion to take over the world' (and you will forever be having to cut it back).

- 'Grandma's favourite' – well, it was until she discovered free-flowering, disease-resistant hybrids.

MULCH ADO

If you dig plenty of organic material into the soil, or mulch around your plants, you can help to conserve moisture and so reduce the need to water. Yes, it will involve extra work in the beginning, but think of the long-term gain!

WATER WELL

You'll be delighted to know that you don't necessarily need to water every night. If you have the kind of garden that consists mostly of established shrubs and trees, they are generally pretty self-sufficient when it comes to water. But even thirstier plants benefit from a more thorough, occasional soaking, rather than a frequent, shallower one, as this encourages the roots to go deeper and makes them less susceptible to drought.

A WORD ABOUT SNAILS

Snails can demolish plants in a trice – these little nasties have been known to strip a lobelia of all its leaves within two days of planting. Sadly, some of the plants that we love for their lush foliage are the same ones that these gastropods view as a gastronomic treat. Slug pellets are out because they are dangerous to pets and wildlife. So unless you're the sort of person who likes to spend their evenings out with a torch checking for snails and disposing of them rather than relaxing with a nice bottle of wine, there is only one answer: just don't grow the plants that they love. OK, so you'll have to forget those visions of lush hostas, the snail's all-time favourite, but just think of the trade-off – you'll be left with more time to relax in your garden, rather than being on constant patrol. You might also avoid plants such as red hot pokers and euphorbias. Gangs of snails like to congregate in their stems, then head out on their nightly raids once the sun is down.

TO HOE . . .

One of the easiest ways to keep down weeds is to hoe. But you will need to do it little and often so that the weeds don't get out of hand.

. . . OR NOT TO HOE

As a deckchair gardener, you'll be delighted to know that there are times when even the hoe should be avoided. In drier spells, disturbing the surface of the soil encourages moisture to evaporate. So when it's hot and dry, leave the hoe in the shed!

KIDS IN THE GARDEN

Introduce children to gardening early and you may be sowing the seeds of a lifetime interest. Choose easy, quick-growing plants to work with. Young children don't have the same concept of time as you and will expect almost instant results! If you think they don't have the patience, you could do the planting out for them, using bedding plants or seedlings. By watching how you do it, they'll be learning a skill too.

POT PEOPLE

Let kids have fun painting funny faces on plant pots, then give them crazy hairstyles with whatever plants they choose to grow in them. They could even do a family of pot people, using different-sized pots. Encourage them to let their imagination run wild. Don't forget that you'll need to supervise young children, both for their safety and your sanity.

For each pot person, you will need:

Terracotta pot and dish
White and coloured water-based paint (acrylic or emulsion)
Paintbrushes
Thick white or greaseproof paper
Pencil
Scissors
Tape
Outdoor varnish
Crocks or stones

Multipurpose compost
Fast-growing seeds or plants for the 'hair'

1 Ask your child to give the pot a coat of white undercoat to cover the terracotta colour, and allow to dry.

2 Next, they should apply two coats of their chosen base colour, leaving time between each coat for the paint to dry.

3 Now ask your child to make a stencil by drawing a face on a piece of paper and cutting out the features (eyes, brows, nose, mouth).

4 Tape the face stencil to the pot and get your child to paint over it.

5 When the paint is dry, carefully remove the stencil. Your child can add more details now – pupils, eyelashes, freckles, whatever grabs their fancy.

6 Varnish the pot to protect the paint, and leave to dry.

7 Put a few crocks or stones in the bottom for drainage, fill with compost, and now for the really fun part – add a plant for the 'hair' or sow some fast-growing seeds. Stand the pot in its dish. Make sure your child remembers to water the 'hair' if they want it to grow.

TOOL KIT

Encourage the gardening habit by giving kids their own child-sized tools. Sets are available in toyshops or larger DIY stores and don't cost too much. Their bright colours are specially chosen to appeal to children. Show them how to look after them – like a grown-up.

BOOT GARDEN

Remember the old nursery rhyme about the old woman who lived in a shoe? Well, why not try a variation on this idea that is bound to amuse kids? Plant up an old pair of wellies, preferably their own!

You will need:

An old wellington boot, or pair of wellies,
brightly coloured and patterned if possible
Stones or broken bits of polystyrene packaging
Three lengths of bamboo cane for each boot
Multipurpose compost
Fast-growing seeds or bedding plants

1 Drill some holes in the soles of the boots to aid drainage.

2 Add some stones or polystyrene packaging to the base, to improve drainage further.

3 Cut three canes to fit inside each leg. They should not show above the top. Insert into the legs to support them.

4 Fill the boots with multipurpose compost.

⑤ Sow some fast-growing seeds in the compost, or plant up with some colourful flowering plants.

YOUNG KITCHEN GARDENER

Introduce children to the idea of growing their own food with these easy edibles.

Radishes are a classic veg for kids to grow because they come up so quickly.

Cress is another easy classic for kids to attempt. The seeds can be grown indoors on kitchen paper or in some shallow compost. The sprouts would even make good 'hair' for a pot person (*see pages 153–4*).

Alfalfa sprouts are fantastic not only because they can be grown easily but because they're also very good for you. Place two tablespoons of alfalfa seeds in a jar and cover with three times their volume of warm water. After eight hours, drain off the excess water and place the jar in a warm place, out of direct sunlight. Rinse the seeds every twelve hours. In about four days, they should have sprouted. Move the jar to a lighter place so that the sprouts can turn green. They are now ready for eating.

RACE FOR THE TOP

Kids will love the challenge of seeing how tall their plants can grow. Try these two surefire winners.

Tallest sunflower

Have a competition to see who can grow the tallest sunflower. They will need to be supported with bamboo canes as they grow. They are extremely easy to grow but in some areas you will need to be on constant slug and snail alert, as sunflowers are a favourite snack. If you are plagued by these monsters, start the plants in pots, off the ground, and only transplant out when they are big and strong enough to withstand attack.

Jack and the beanstalk

The story of Jack and his beanstalk will add a bit of extra magic to this activity – and it's a real lesson in botany too. Place some runner bean seeds between layers of damp kitchen paper or cotton wool on a dish or saucer. Keep them damp and in a few days they will have sprouted. Gently lift the covering to show the kids the miraculous way the seeds have suddenly come alive, with the radical (the root) going one way and the shoot (the part that will form the stem) going the other. Carefully transfer the sprouted seeds to pots and, when the seedlings are big enough, transplant them to larger pots or the ground. Give them canes to grow up and help the children to measure them regularly to see how much they have grown.

PAINT A MURAL

You need considerable artistic skill to paint a convincing mural so why not go 'naïve' and paint a garden mural with the kids? It won't be pretending to be great art but it will have a lot of charm, and the kids will love doing it.

FAMOUS GARDENERS

Nature provides the plants. Humans create the gardens. Here are just a handful of celebrated individuals who have taken Nature's bounty and sculpted it to make gardens to delight the senses.

André Le Nôtre (1613–1700)
Gardener to France's King Louis XIV from 1645 to 1700, Le Nôtre was responsible for the park at the Palace of Versailles, his most famous creation. His style was formal and included parterres, a type of garden that uses planting, such as low, tightly clipped hedging, to create symmetrical patterns.

Capability Brown (1715–83)
Lancelot 'Capability' Brown was an English landscape gardener whose romantic, naturalistic style contrasted with the formalism of Le Nôtre. He got his nickname because of his enthusiasm for the 'capabilities' of natural landscapes. Characterized by sweeping vistas and broad lakes punctuated by clusters of trees and classical follies, his parks include those of the grandest English country houses, such as Stowe (his first commission at the age of twenty-six), Blenheim Palace and Chatsworth House.

Thomas Jefferson (1743–1826)
A love of gardening even extended to the US presidency. Thomas Jefferson, the third President of the United States (1801–1809) and principal author of the American Declaration of Independence (1776), was an avid gardener and horticulturist.

*No occupation is so delightful to me as the culture of the
earth, no culture comparable to that of the garden . . . But
though an old man, I am but a young gardener.*
THOMAS JEFFERSON, *GARDEN BOOK*

Claude Monet (1840–1926)

After Monet, a leading French Impressionist painter, bought
his house at Giverny in northern France in 1890, he turned
his painter's eye to the land around it, creating natural-looking,
flower-filled gardens and water-lily ponds that became the subject
of some of his most famous paintings, including his *Water Lilies*
series. Monet lived in Giverny from 1883 until his death.

*There is no spot of ground, however arid, bare or ugly, that
cannot be tamed into such a state as may give an impression
of beauty and delight.*
GERTRUDE JEKYLL

Gertrude Jekyll (1843–1932)

Another painter, Gertrude Jekyll (pronounced 'jee-kul') also had
the advantage of an artist's eye and used flowering plants like
paints to create splashes of colour, rather like an Impressionist
using a brush. A highly influential British garden designer,
she created more than 400 gardens in the United Kingdom,

Europe and the United States. A member of the Arts and Crafts movement, she designed many gardens for the houses designed by Edwin Lutyens, an architect with whom she worked closely.

Vita Sackville-West (1892–1962)

An English novelist, poet and member of the Bloomsbury Group, Vita Sackville-West is best remembered for the garden she created at Sissinghurst Castle in Kent in the south of England, in the 1930s. She lived here with her husband, the author and diplomat Harold Nicolson, and made Sissinghurst famous through her regular gardening column for the *Observer* newspaper. The garden is characterized by a series of 'rooms' divided by high, clipped hedges and walls, each with its own character in colour and theme.

It isn't that I don't like sweet disorder, but it has to be judiciously arranged.
VITA SACKVILLE-WEST